How Dependable Is the Bible?

EVANGELICAL PERSPECTIVES
John Warwick Montgomery, General Editor

How Black Is the Gospel?
by Tom Skinner

The Unequal Yoke
by Richard V. Pierard

God, Sex and You
by M. O. Vincent, M.D.

Revolution and the Christian Faith
by Vernon C. Grounds

How Dependable Is the Bible?
by Raymond F. Surburg

The Stones and the Scriptures
by Edwin M. Yamauchi

How Dependable Is the Bible?

RAYMOND F. SURBURG

J. B. Lippincott Company
Philadelphia and New York / A HOLMAN BOOK

U.S. Library of Congress Cataloging in Publication Data

Surburg, Raymond F   birth date
  How Dependable Is the Bible?

  (Evangelical perspectives)
  "A Holman book."
  Bibliography: p.
  1. Bible—Evidences, authority, etc. 2. Bible
—Criticism, interpretation, etc. I. Title.
BS480.S77   220.1   75-39707

  ISBN-0-87981-003-3

Foreword
A Perspective on "Evangelical Perspectives"

Across the centuries the Christian church has faced two perennial challenges: the maintenance of a pure testimony, and the application of revealed truth to the total life of man. Though these two tasks interlock (since application of the truth is impossible if the truth is lost, and truth without application stands self-condemned), theology has generally devoted itself now to the one, now to the other, and the cause of Christ has suffered from the imbalance. "These ought ye to have done, and not to leave the other undone" stands as a perpetual judgment over the church's history.

Today's theology and church life display such deleterious polarization in an especially gross manner. At the liberal end of the theological spectrum, efforts to become "relevant" have succeeded so well that the church has become indistinguishable from the ideological and societal evils she is supposed to combat. Among the fundamentalists, in contrast, God's revealed truth often serves as a wall to block the church off from the live issues and compelling challenges of a world in crisis.

5

How Dependable Is the Bible?

Relevance without truth, or truth without relevance: these dual schizophrenias go far in explaining why contemporary man finds it easy to ignore the Christian message.

Evangelical Perspectives is a series of books designed specifically to overcome these false dichotomies. Historic Christian theology—the Christianity of the Apostles' Creed, of the Protestant Reformation, and of the eighteenth-century Evangelical Revival—is taken with full seriousness, and is shown to be entirely compatible with the best of contemporary scholarship. Contributors to this series are united in rejecting the defensive posture which has so often created the impression that new knowledge poses a genuine threat to the Christian gospel. Axiomatic to the present series is the conviction that new discoveries serve but to confirm and deepen the faith once delivered to the saints.

At the same time, those participating in this project find little comfort in the reiteration of ancient truth for its own sake. Our age faces staggering challenges which can hardly be met by the repetition of formulas—certainly not by the negativistic codes of a fundamentalism which tilts against windmills that have long since fallen into decay. The race problem, social revolution, political change, new sexual freedom, the revival of the occult, the advent of the space age: these are areas of modern life that demand fresh analysis on the basis of the eternal verities set forth in the Word of One who is the same yesterday, today, and forever.

Out of the flux of the current theological situation nothing but flux appears to be emerging. What is needed is a firm foundation on which to build an all-embracing and genuinely relevant theological perspective for the emerging twenty-first century. The authors of the present volumes are endeavoring to offer just such a perspective—an *evangelical* perspective, a perspective arising from the biblical evangel—as the one path through the maze of contemporary life.

It is the hope of the editor that upon the solid Reformation base of a fully authoritative Scripture, the present series will offer its readers the Renaissance ideal of the Christian as *uomo universale*. Such an orientation could revolutionize theology in our time, and ground a new age of commitment and discovery comparable to that of the sixteenth century. As in that day, new worlds are opening up, and just as a religious viewpoint reflecting the dying medieval age was unable to meet the challenge then, so today's secular theologies are incapable of pointing the way now. The Christ of the Bible, through whom all without exception have been created and redeemed: He alone is Way, Truth, Life—and Perspective!

John Warwick Montgomery
General Editor

Contents

1
Who's Listening?

If the only Bibles available to twentieth century Americans were the church-approved Latin manuscripts of the Middle Ages, the widespread lack of biblical knowledge would not be surprising. But while the Bible continuously tops the best seller list and is available in printed versions varying from children's picture Bibles, to paperbacks in teen lingo, to modern English translations and paraphrases, to scholarly editions including cross referencing and concordances, and to tape recordings of Scripture for use by the blind, the general public remains appallingly ignorant of even simple Bible stories. In 1906 Prof. Edgar Work, in his volume entitled, *The Fascination of the Book,* asserted: "The wealth and the resources of the Bible have not been fully enough exposed. It is to be sure, always the Book of the people, yet multitudes are holding it at arm's length instead of admitting it into close fellowship of interest."[1]

Army chaplains during the two World Wars found themselves in the awkward position of dealing with men facing death who knew little of God's Word and His provision for man. One World War I chaplain claimed that the Bible was

11

the "book nobody knows." During World War II chaplains again bewailed the lack of knowledge of elementary Bible facts and bemoaned the fact that for millions the Bible was like a sealed book. Many soldiers who owned Bibles merely used them as talismans or carried them in their bags out of sentimental attachment.

In the early history of America the Scripture was often used as a primer as well as for devotional reading in the schools. Children were thus exposed to the Bible and its teachings if only because few other books were available.

As the country grew and prospered however, other educational materials replaced the Bible in the schools. In recent years the fears of sectarian teaching, unscientific indoctrination, and various interpretations of the constitutional provision for the separation of church and state have proscribed the use of the Bible in our public schools. It is more than ironic that the book which has changed lives, caused men to die martyrs' deaths, was a major factor in the Protestant Reformation and contains some of the world's greatest literature, is steadfastly ignored in the name of education. Dr. Wilbur White, leader in methodology in Bible study and founder of the old Biblical Seminary, correctly asserted: "The Bible cannot be studied apart from history. Produced by life, it in turn has made everyone live whithersoever it has gone. And yet we exclude the Bible from education! Is there any need of support of our proposition and our protest."[2] Since it has played such an important role in Western civilization, the Bible cannot, on good pedagogical grounds, be ignored.

The home is the greatest and most important agency for education. Yet it is a rarity even among Christians, when an entire family regularly reads and studies Scripture together. "Already within easy possession of everyone lies a guide that is dependable, inexhaustible, unchanging. For the answers to our children's questions this is one indispensable source of wisdom and authority," writes Martha Leavell. She continues, "Children and youth need instruction and training in Bible reading, in the devotional use of Scripture, in memory work and in guidelines for Christian living based upon God's Word."[3] But many parents have abdicated their duty to train their children in the nurture and wisdom of the Lord, assuming perhaps, that the Sunday school can accomplish this with one hour each week.

Unfortunately many Sunday school teachers, youth leaders and pastors are as ignorant of the Word of God as the average agnostic. While we vigorously guard against incompetence in the professions and insist on qualified, capable public school teachers, we blithely send our children to Sunday school classes and youth meetings, unmindful of the teacher's knowledge of the Bible or skill in communicating. And in many Protestant churches the Bible is simply not taught at all.

Even in the seminaries, the Bible is neglected. Twenty years ago Dr. Howard Kuist said of students entering theological seminaries, "It can no longer be assumed that a student brings to his seminary training a general knowledge of the English Bible."[4] Most students enrolling are woefully deficient in general Bible knowledge; and in many cases that deficiency is never removed. At many seminaries there are courses about the Bible, and much time is devoted to practical courses in preaching, Christian education and counseling. But the students leave the seminary poorly equipped with firsthand Bible knowledge. With the elimination of Bible courses from much of the modern theological curricula, seminary graduates are not prepared for the professional ministry. The result is that many young pastors enter their fields of labor not knowing much of God's Book which they are supposed to expound and apply in life situations.

With biblically ignorant pastors and teachers is it any wonder that many Protestant churches are spiritually handicapped? In addressing the elders of Ephesus Paul offered a solution for this kind of weakness: "I commend you to God and to the word of his grace, which is able to build you up, and to give you an inheritance among all them which are sanctified" (Acts 20:32). God expects spiritual growth on the part of Christian people; and spiritual immaturity can be attributed to neglect of the Scriptures. "Grow in grace and the knowledge of our Lord and Savior Jesus Christ" (II Pet. 3:18). Christ promised His followers: "If ye continue in my word, then are ye my disciples indeed and ye shall know the truth and the truth shall make you free" (John 8:32).

Dr. I.T. Watts, a former leader of the Southern Baptist Convention expressed the view that the Church's ignorance of the Bible was a definite hindrance to the great missionary effort of the Church universal. It is only as people read the greatest missionary book in the world that they will derive inspiration and incentive and thus be motivated to follow the great commission of Christ and to support the missionary program of the Church.

Neglect of the Bible as we have it today is a great national peril. The last United States census indicated that more than fifty percent of America's population is completely outside of the Christian Church and its Book. It was Daniel Webster who said: "If we abide by the principles taught in the Bible we will go on to prosper; but if we and our posterity neglect its instruction and authority, no man can tell how sudden a catastrophe may overwhelm us and bury all our glory in profound obscurity."[5] The cup of God's

14

wrath will surely be poured out upon a nation that neglects the Bible and its teachings.

How did it happen that the Bible, which occupied an important place in the early history of our land, has become relegated to the back seat or in many instances has been completely neglected and discredited ?

The theory of evolution and its corollary social implications has influenced many religious scholars, resulting in the claims of traditional Christianity being relinquished. Instead of regarding the Bible as a divine-human book, such scholars have debased it to the level of any human book.

Another contributing factor in the relegation of the Bible to a place of little importance is humanistic philosophy. Dr. John Dewey rejected Christianity and substituted a humanistic paganism which places man, instead of God, at the center of life. In his book, *The Quest for Certainty*, Dewey encouraged individuals to reject the restrictive ideas and ideals of the past and to build a new order in which there is no distinction between the temporal and the eternal. The Dewey philosophy has received wide acceptance, especially in American educational theory.

Another factor in the decline of the Bible's influence was the introduction of various forms of biblical criticism which question the reliability, accuracy and authority of the Bible, into theological seminaries and departments of religion at colleges and universities. Dr. Clarence Benson has asserted about one educational institution: "As the members for the most part had modernistic conceptions of the Bible, their contributions were at variance with those who accepted the Scriptures in their entirety as the Word of God."[6]

[6]Used by permission. Moody Press, Moody Bible Institute of Chicago.

How Dependable Is the Bible?

Another prominent religious organization has advocated methods and types of research that are hostile to the educational and doctrinal teachings of the Bible. Frequently human solutions to social problems are substituted for the Word of God.

Modernism, a theological belief that questions the Bible's supernatural character, denies the Scripture's miracles, the deity of Christ and other fundamental teachings, is also responsible for a decline in the use of the Bible. Theological liberalism, rampant during the first three decades of this century, attacked the foundation of our faith by professing to be a friend of the Bible.

A reaction to theological liberalism set in between 1930 and 1940 in America under the guise of a movement variously referred to as neoorthodoxy, neosupernaturalism, or "theology of the Word." In some respects this new movement reaffirmed theological doctrines that had been held by historic Christianity and repudiated by modernism. However, neoorthodoxy's use of the historical critical method together with its unwillingness to accept the Bible as the inspired revelation of God, led to the sponsoring of views that are just as destructive to the Bible as were those of the movement it reacted against. The critical use of the Bible and the adoption of principles of interpretation that are not in harmony with the clear assertions of Scripture have resulted in a questioning of the reliability of the Bible as a guide in matters of doctrine and ethics. The hermeneutical principles used by neoorthodox scholars has resulted in a rejection of many biblical doctrines and a refusal to accept the Bible's own claim to be God's guide book for all people for this life, and the only volume that can prepare them for a happy eternity.

Negative higher criticism has been employed in the study

16

of the Scriptures and has resulted in a weakening of biblical teaching and the discrediting of its truths. In view of the teachings that have questioned the veracity and reliability of the Bible, twentieth century man naturally wonders whether the Bible can still be trusted as a reliable religious guide. Because of the many and varied onslaughts made upon the integrity, historicity and reliability of the sixty-six books of the Scripture, must the Bible surrender its binding message for the person of today?

It is to these problems that the following chapters of this book will address themselves. The author will set forth the various types of biblical criticism in vogue today, examine their presuppositions, note the methodology employed in dealing with Scriptures and evaluate the conclusions to determine whether or not today's biblical reader can still place the same trust in the Bible, as did believers of former generations, and hold that the Bible is a dependable book.

2
What Is Valid
Biblical Criticism?

The Bible is actually a library, a collection of sixty-six different books written over a period of sixteen hundred years. The language in which the Old Testament books were written was Hebrew with the exception of half of Daniel and portions of Ezra which were written also in biblical Aramaic; both languages belong to the Semitic language family. The books of the New Testament have come down to us in Koine Greek, one of the better known Indo-European languages. At least thirty-five different writers were involved in composing the books now regarded as the Sacred Scriptures by those who designate themselves Christians.

None of the original writings either of the Old or New Testaments has survived. At least eighteen hundred years have elapsed between the last New Testament writing and the present time. In the case of the first books of the Old Testament the time gap is over thirty-four hundred years. Since the biblical writings are products of the Near East and Graeco-Roman worlds, there are references in these books which were perfectly clear to their first recipients but which present difficulties of understanding for twentieth century readers. Because of different types of gaps, linguistic and cultural, existing between the original writers and those of today, the need for interpretation is necessary. The biblical reader needs to acquaint himself with the principles of interpretation, technically called hermeneutics. In applying the rules of hermeneutics the biblical interpreter practices what is known by the theological term as "exegesis." Historical criticism and philological criticism are a part of hermeneutics and will not be discussed in this book. It is impossible to understand the contents of the Bible without the use of biblical criticism. Many Christians when they hear the word "criticism" applied to the Bible at once conjure up negative concepts.

However, in itself the word "critical" does not necessarily mean, "judgmental." The word criticism comes from the Greek word "krisis" which simply means judgment or the art of judgment to make an analysis of merits or faults. Biblical criticism refers to the scholarly as opposed to a slovenly arbitrary or misguided method in dealing with the literature of the Scriptures. Appropriately Ramm wrote about the word "critical":

The word critical is an abused word. To those who confuse principles of piety with principles of scholarship, the word is equated with skepticism. By critical we mean that any interpretation of Scripture must have adequate justification, the grounds for the interpretation *must be made explicit!*[1]

It cannot be denied, however, that often that which claims to be unbiased and objective criticism of the Bible is judgmental and destructive of the truths of the Scriptures.

Biblical criticism may be defined as the application to biblical writings of certain techniques used in the examination of many kinds of literature in order to establish as far as possible their original wording, the manner and date of their composition, their sources, authorship and so forth. Scholars have distinguished a number of different types of criticism: textual, literary, form criticism, redaction criticism and *Sachkritik* (content criticism).

1. Textual Criticism

Textual criticism is concerned with the investigation of the changes in the course of hand copying and recopying that have occurred in a document for the purpose of restoring it to its original form (the autographs). Even in printing, despite a book being examined by a number of proofreaders, mistakes occur in printed materials. The task of the textual critic is not an easy one but of primary importance. When a writer's original production is accessible, correcting errors that have been made in printing is relatively simple by comparison with the autographs. However, when an original composition has been lost or destroyed and is no longer available, restoration of the original text is difficult, requiring considerable effort to obtain the original wording. The methods and procedures of the science of textual criticism were first used in connection with the study of classical texts and from that field were appropriated to the restoration of the text of the New Testament. Because of their high reverence for the Sacred Scriptures, Christian scholars should be especially interested in biblical textual criticism. To become a competent textual critic much knowledge and preparation are required and proficiency in this art cannot be acquired in haste.

Variant readings are found in biblical manuscripts as the result of centuries of copying and recopying and they may be classified as variations made involuntarily and those made deliberately. Corrections of the former kind have been called verbal criticism and those of the latter, material criticism.

All books that have been transmitted to us from ancient times have suffered from copyists' mistakes. Some kinds of mistakes that occur in Hebrew and Greek manuscripts are: confusion of letters having nearly the same form (mistakes made by the eyes), or words having the same sound (errors made by the ear when the text was dictated). These mistakes happened especially when proper names and numbers were written or dictated. Other common mistakes are the addition, omission and transposition of letters, syllables, or words, and even of phrases or clauses. In ancient manuscripts there was no separation between words but continuous script; the result is that in later copies wrong words were sometimes combined. Around 700 A.D. when the Massoretes vocalized the consonantal Hebrew text, the consonants were sometimes given the wrong vowels. The Massoretes also changed the meaning of certain verses by the introduction of a defective accentuation and thus a wrong interpretation was given to a passage.

The science of textual criticism has been able to classify the types of errors that scribes made and which are found repeatedly in all manuscripts. Among commonly repeated errors are the following: haplography, that is, the failure to repeat a letter or a word; dittography, the tendency to repeat what only occurs once; false recollection, when a scribe copies a passage similar in another manuscript or when he records what he has memorized incorrectly. Another type of common error is known as hemoeteleuton, the omission of a passage between identical words. The opposite error would be the repetition of the same lines that occur near similar words. Notes that were originally found in the margin of a text sometimes were copied into the text itself.

In copies of the Greek New Testament the phenomenon known as iotacism or substitution of vowels which were pronounced in the same way was practiced.

The study of comparative texts can lead to the elimination of many textual corruptions. However, the preponderance of manuscripts is not decisive for the establishment of a reliable text because several representatives of the same archetype count only as one witness to the text.

2. Literary Criticism

To distinguish literary criticism from lower or textual criticism, the study of books as literary documents is designated "higher criticism." After the best possible text has been established by lower or textual criticism the biblical student is then in a position to ask certain questions of a given biblical book: Who wrote it? Why did the author write the book in the form we have it? To whom is it addressed? Under what circumstances was it written? From what time does it come? What sources, if any, did the author use? These are questions dating back to the early Christian centuries that students of the Sacred Scriptures have been asking of each biblical book. The term "higher criticism" was first applied by J.G. Eichorn in the preface to the second edition of his *Old Testament Introduction* (1787). In this edition Eichorn claimed that it was necessary for him to devote a great deal of labor in a field hitherto completely unworked which involved the investigation of the inner structure of individual Old Testament books by means of higher criticism—not a new name for a humanist.

Biblical writers sometimes made use of other written sources in writing their books. Thus I and II Chronicles refer to many sources which were ascribed to prophets. Scholars believe that the Books of Samuel and the Books of

Kings are two major sources referred to by the author of Chronicles. The Book of Jashar and the Book of the Wars of the Lord are alluded to in other Old Testament books. The author of Kings refers to three different historical sources which may have been court annals.

In the area of New Testament studies an hypothesis was put forward that Matthew and Luke had employed the Gospel of Mark as a basic source and that another source "Q" contained material that Mark did not have but which Matthew and Luke have in common. The "Q" source has never been found nor is it referred to in any ancient book. It is a construct of literary critics.

Where sources are not designated nor mentioned in any of the scriptural books and there are no references extant in patristic ecclesiastical literature, the postulation of sources for scriptural books presents a great problem. This is a fact which many biblical students have not recognized. For example, as Bruce has pointed out, if today we only had Tatian's harmony of the four Gospels called Diatessaron, arranged about 170 A.D., and scholars had to separate the four Gospels on the basis of this work, it would be practically impossible to separate them. It might be possible to disentangle the Synoptic materials from the Johannine but it would be absolutely impossible to distinguish the documents that belong to the Synoptic writers since all three have in common many events and sayings of Christ's life. This is the situation that confronts students of the Pentateuch who believe that they can separate the documents that allegedly comprised the Pentateuch. There is agreement among critical scholars that a number of documents underly the present Pentateuch, but how many documents are to be found is the great question the critics have not been able to answer. Nor have they been able to state where one document begins and the other ends. Today there is more uncertainty over the number and extent of the sources in the Pentateuch than there was at the beginning of the twentieth century.

Biblical criticism utilizes internal and external evidence in dating a biblical document. Conservative biblical criticism would hold that if references to the Pentateuch are found in books coming from the eighth century it would mean that the Pentateuch was in existence before the time referred to or quoted. Since Micah 3:12 (announcing the destruction of Jerusalem) is referred to in Jeremiah 26 it presupposes the prior existence of the prophet Micah's book. Some parts of Old Testament history can be dated because in Egyptian and Babylonian history there are references to historical personages and events mentioned in various Old Testament writings. In the prophetical writings of the Old Testament, references are often cited when an oracle was given, or the reign or reigns during which the prophet uttered his preaching or predictions. As archaeology has been making the history of the Near East known in greater detail, Old Testament history is better understood in its Near Eastern milieu.

Among biblical critics a difference of opinion exists about the possibility of predictive prophecy. Those literary critics who accept the supernatural have no difficulty in believing that the prophets, who functioned under the guidance of God, could announce events years in advance of their actual occurrence. On the other hand, those critics who deny the fact that God made his will known to His "servants, the prophets" will interpret all fulfilled prophecy as *vaticinia ex eventu* (i.e. happenings after the event). Thus conservative scholars would date Habakkuk some time before the year 612 B.C., the date for the fall of Nineveh, which had been predicted by the Prophet Nahum, but later than the fall of Thebes in 663 B.C., an event alluded to by the same prophet (3:8ff). The exact time for the writing of Nahum would have to be determined by a careful interpretation of the three chapters of Nahum.

In Old Testament studies the dominant critical problem is that of the authorship and composition of the Pentateuch. The beginning of Pentateuchal criticism began with H.B. Witter and especially J. Astruc (1753), who postulated twelve different sources in the Book of Genesis, two being distinguished by means of the names Yahweh and Elohim. J.G. Eichorn was responsible for extending the existence of the use of Yahweh and Elohim as indicative of different sources to the entire Pentateuch. De Wette in 1805 proposed the idea of making the Book of Deuteronomy a separate source that had its origin in the seventh century B.C. Geddes and Vater proposed many smaller units and came up with the fragmentary hypothesis. Ewald proposed the Supplementary theory according to which "E" was the main document (*Grundschrift*) and "J" was used to supplement the so-called *Grundschrift* (foundation source). H. Hupfeld distinguished two sources in Astruc's original "E" source which Hupfeld called "E1" and "E2," and "E1" was renamed the "P" source now considered to be the youngest of the four basic sources that eventually were recognized by critical Old Testament scholarship.

With Julius Wellhausen the Documentary Hypothesis reached its culmination. In addition to popularizing the acceptance of the four sources in the order of "J" (850 B.C.), "E" (750 B.C.), "D" (621 B.C.), and "P" (450 B.C.), he also promoted the idea of the evolutionary development of religion. The documentary sources were correlated with the developmental concept and an interpretation of the data of

25

the Old Testament was given which placed the prophetic movement before the giving of the Law and the existence of the priestly class. Archaeological discoveries, which Wellhausen ignored, have disproved most of Wellhausen's positions.

The division of the Pentateuch into different documents has led to the same critical principles being applied to other books of the Old Testament. Practically every book of the Old Testament has been assigned to more than one source or author. The Book of Isaiah is said to have at least three or more authors; in fact, critics speak of Isaiah as the product of a school of writers who between 750 B.C. and 250 B.C. wrote and gathered together the sixty-six chapters found in the present biblical book. Jeremiah, to cite another example, is alleged to have at least three different authors, and Zechariah at least four different authors who are said to have written the chapters that comprise the present biblical text.

The New Testament
In New Testament studies the dominant critical issue has been the Synoptic problem. How are the first three Gospels related to each other? It was C. Lachmann (1835) who proposed the theory that Mark was the earliest Gospel which was used by Matthew and Luke. Bultmann has tried to find various sources in the fourth gospel but his theory has not won the approval of other New Testament critical scholars.

In New Testament studies the Pauline Epistles have played a role comparable to that of the Pentateuch in the field of Old Testament studies. F.C. Bauer (1831), like Wellhausen, applied the Hegelian philosophy of history to the Pauline letters. Bauer only recognized Romans, I and II

Corinthians and Galatians as genuinely Pauline. Paul's letters were placed in opposition to those of Peter. The clash between the Pauline group and the Petrine party is supposed to have resulted in early Catholic Christianity. The Book of Acts and other later New Testament writings are presumed to reflect this synthesis which resulted from the discord between the thesis (Paul) and the antithesis (Peter). The Dutch New Testament scholar W.C. van Manen (1890) considered all Pauline Letters unauthentic. This radical position failed to win adherents, while the Tübingen School was rejected by such English biblical critics as J.B. Lightfoot, B.F. Westcott and William Sanday.

3. Form Criticism

Form criticism was proposed both by Old Testament and New Testament scholars as a new critical approach to biblical literature. Because in the opinion of Gunkel, source criticism was unsatisfactory, he used insights that were provided by students of Norse, Germanic and Slavonic literature. Gunkel adopted the idea that in the Near East as in Greece and other lands, literature is supposed to have existed in oral form centuries before it was committed to writing. Gunkel set forth the idea that the prehistory of the text must be studied in order to determine the different types of literary genre of which it was composed. Gunkel also held that it was important to determine the life situation (*Sitz-im-Leben*) for each type of literary genre. After the small literary units had been determined, the next step was to find out how the smaller literary units were combined into tradition cycles. Gunkel initially developed his approach with the book of Genesis in his *Legends of Genesis.* Herein he explains the techniques applied to this biblical book which, according to Gunkel, contains different types of legends, thereby completely denying the historical character of the episodes in chapters 1-11 and also seriously questioning the patriarchal narratives found in chapters 12-50 of Genesis. Later Gunkel applied form criticism to the poetic literature of the Old Testament. His classification of the Psalms has become famous and Gunkel exercised a great influence on Psalm studies in the twentieth century in Europe and America.

Scandinavian scholars led by Engnell, Nyberg, Mowinckel and Nielsen, called the Uppsala School, stressed oral tradition, claiming that the Documentary Hypothesis popularized by Wellhausen was wrong and that the Old Testament was not written prior to the Babylonian Captivity (587 B.C.). The Scandinavian School rejected the traditional Four Documentary Hypothesis and assumed that Old Testament history was handed down orally in large blocks of tradition which did not change in the course of the centuries prior to 539 B.C..In this respect the position of the Uppsala School contradicted the position of Gunkel who believed that new life situations resulted in the changing of the traditions passed on from previous times.

In the New Testament area, form criticism was applied to the Gospels from 1919 onwards. Edgar Krentz has described this methodology as follows:

Form criticism investigates the forms and patterns in ancient literature in order to set them into their place in the history of literature and to determine the cultural or religious setting that originally produced and used the form (*Sitz-im-Leben*). It seeks to work back from the text to the setting of the original core of a literary form by defining and removing the later additions, modifications, made in the oral period and by the literary editor who arranged the material into a consecutive literary document.[2]

[2]*Biblical Studies Today.* Krentz, Edgar, 1966, Concordia Publishing House. Used by permission of the publisher.

What Is Valid Biblical Criticism?

Form criticism emphasized the following as presuppositions of its methodology: 1. The Gospels in our present manuscripts are not the single creations out of a whole cloth but consist of collections of material, the final selection and arrangement of which we owe to the evangelists themselves. 2. The present Gospels have a prehistory in terms of oral transmission. Small collections or related materials are supposed to have been circulated in the early church where they were used for preaching or catechetical instruction. 3. The small oral tradition units were classified as follows: pronouncement stories, miracle stories, and sayings (subdivided as wisdom words, parables, myths, legends). The various form critics are by no means agreed as to these classifications. The form critics seek to remove the original form of the story or saying by stripping it of its traditional accretions and of the editorial additions made by the evangelists. Following this procedure the form critic seeks to establish the *Sitz-im-Leben* (life situation) of a pericope; trying to determine for what purpose, or to meet what needs, the first church supposedly preserved, shaped, or invented this or that story or saying.

Students of the form critical approach to the Gospels claim that hidden behind the assumptions of this methodology are the ghosts of Gunkel, Wrede and Wellhausen. Redlich, one of the authorities in the field of form criticism wrote: "It is to the doubts of the historical value of Mark that we ultimately owe the coming of Form Criticism."[3] Form criticism which aims at examining the oral Gospel assumes that the various forms were creations of the Christian community. If this assumption is correct it would mean that the Gospels tell us more about the church that created the various forms of literature than they tell us about the sayings and deeds of Jesus.

29

How Dependable Is the Bible?

Form criticism has led to skepticism concerning the sayings and deeds of Jesus. It has questioned the historical reliability of the facts recorded in the four Gospels. An examination of the writings of Bultmann, Schmidt and Dibelius shows major disagreements about their use of the method. Dr. Franzmann made the following evaluation of form criticism: "It is scholarly heresy to say so, but one wonders whether the church of God is well served by any of these attempts to penetrate into the substrata of the Gospels which it has pleased God to give to His Church. All of the theories must, in view of the paucity of the evidence, remain highly speculative. None of them in the last analysis contributes much to the understanding of the Gospels as we have them."[4]

4. Redaction Criticism

Redaction criticism is another discipline within the historical critical method, one that has become prominent during the last twenty years. It grew out of form criticism and is closely associated with the study of the Gospels. Norman Perrin has written a monograph entitled *What Is Form Criticism?* wherein he has shown the development of this latest type of criticism.

Via claims that redaction criticism "presupposes and continues the procedures of the earlier discipline (form criticism) while extending and intensifying certain of them."[5] While form criticism and redaction criticism are two aspects of one unified discipline, redaction criticism presents enough of a divergence to justify a separate treatment in the eyes of its proponents. The backgrounds of redaction criticism are traced back to critical scholars like

[4]*The Word of the Lord Grows.* Franzmann, Martin R. 1961, Concordia Publishing House. Used by permission of the publisher.

Reimarus, Strauss, Holtzmann, Wrede, Wellhausen, Dibelius, Schmidt and Bultmann. According to Perrin:

Redaction criticism is particularly concerned with studying the theological motivation of an author as this is revealed in the collection, arrangement, editing, and modification of traditional material, and in the composition of the new material or the creation of new forms within the traditions of early Christianity.[6]

Tradition criticism strives to understand why items about Jesus as they were transmitted were modified and connected in the manner as found in the Gospels. This new form of criticism also wishes to identify the motifs that were operative in the composition of the completed Gospel, and to explain the theological viewpoint that is expressed in and throughout the book. Redaction criticism, therefore, might also be called "composition criticism."

As will be shown later in this book the evangelists are not to be considered merely transmitters of traditions which they had received (as in the case of Mark and Luke) or recorders of what they actually heard and saw (Matthew and John) but the Gospels' writers created events and ascribed sayings to Jesus in the interest of formulating a theology. If the presuppositions and conclusions of redaction criticism are accepted, then it will be an impossibility for scholars to write a life of Jesus. It would seriously invalidate the search for the sayings of Jesus if the first three Gospels' writers actually created Jesus' sayings and ascribed them to Him.

Both form criticism and redaction criticism have serious implications for the study of the Gospels and their adoption could result in the Church being uncertain about most of its christological teachings. Those who practice these types of criticism can only bring about a spirit of skepticism regarding Jesus Christ, the Savior and Redeemer of mankind. These forms of literary criticism are subversive and tend to undermine the foundations of the Christian faith!

5. Sachkritik (Content criticism)

Another form of criticism practiced by biblical scholars is *Sachkritik* or content criticism which involves theological criticism of the contents of a biblical book. This is an extremely subjective form of criticism and one that is destructive of the biblical teachings. Thus various New Testament scholars will evaluate a book in terms of whether or not the doctrine of justification by faith is taught. Others will evaluate a writing in the light of what they believe the situation should have demanded. Theological criticism also passes on what books should be considered canonical and which not.

3
Biblical Criticism throughout the Ages

The earliest Christians were not agitated or disturbed over biblical questions as Christians of the twentieth century. Jesus and His disciples attended the synagogue services where the Pentateuch and the Prophets were read in Hebrew followed by Aramaic paraphrases which were later written down and known as Targums. Somewhere between 250 and 130 B.C. the Hebrew text of the Old Testament was translated into Greek. There was no doubt in the minds of Gentile Christians that the Septuagint translation did accurately reflect the Hebrew and Aramaic texts of the Old Testament. St. Justin is an example in his *Dialogues with Trypho* of how the first Christians could argue ingeniously from the Septuagint.

Studies by twentieth century scholars show that the value once attributed to the Septuagint cannot be maintained. Thus G. Bardy has shown that the Septuagint was an uneven translation and that there is no compelling reason to believe that the Septuagint was made under a single direction. It is probable that the Pentateuch was translated first and was highly respected by the Jews. The historical books are equally good translations. However, the poetical and prophetical books do not match the quality of the Pentateuch. As a version the Septuagint is uneven and mediocre and, according to the analysis of Vaccari, is a translation that is not adequate from any point of view. Some of the translators of individual books knew little Hebrew and were not skilled in Greek composition. Other books seem to have been done as private translations and were not prepared for liturgical use as was the Pentateuch.

Alexandria in Egypt developed into the intellectual capital of the Greek-speaking people of the Roman Empire. The city founded by Alexander became the home of the renowned library established by the Ptolemies, and the seat of a famous school of textual criticism was located there. It was not unnatural that after the spread of Christianity that a school for the study of the Bible was founded here. In the year 185 A.D. Origen was born who was to become known as "the first textual critic." When Origen began to employ the rules of textual criticism to the Septuagint he was not inventing something new, but was merely employing traditional principles for establishing a text that he had learned from his masters with whom he had studied the Greek pagan classics.

Origen became concerned about the Septuagintal text which in his day was suffering from textual corruptions and changes. He produced a monumental work, believed to have embraced fifty volumes, in which a page was devoted to each word of the Septuagintal text. This work is known as the *Hexapla,* a polyglot Bible having six columns. In the first column Origen placed the Hebrew text, which he then transliterated in Greek letters in the second column. The other four columns contained three other Greek translations together with his own critical text of what he believed should be the true Septuagintal text. First came Aquila's translation, which was extremely literal; next to it was the revision of Symmachus in a Greek that was most elegant, and in the sixth column was Theodotian's translation, which was nothing more than a revision of the Septuagint translation corrected by Aquila's version. In the fifth column Origen placed the text of the Septuagint revised by himself. His method of revision was to choose from the Greek manuscripts available to him, the readings nearest the Hebrew text current in his day. Where his reconstruction did not have any text as compared with the Hebrew, he inserted words and marked them by critical signs; where his text contained readings that Hebrew did not have, he kept them but placed them in parentheses. Finally the order of the Greek text was so altered so that it would agree with the Hebrew. It was estimated that the *Hexapla* must have been a work of considerable size, embracing about 6,500 pages. The complete work was placed in the library at Caesarea in Palestine. When the Moslems conquered Palestine, Caesarea was destroyed. A palimpsest of the Psalms was found in 1896 and preserves five leaves from the *Hexapla*. Origen adopted a method of interpretation that has been labeled as allegorical. His method of hermeneutics consisted in finding a hidden meaning behind the literal sense. By means of allegory and spiritualizing he was able to evade the literal meaning of the text. Today his method of interpretation would be considered artificial and erroneous.

The Western church was slow to recognize the need for biblical criticism. Latin-speaking Christians used a number of different Latin translations. These Latin translations can be placed into two classes: European, used in the churches of Rome, and African, employed at Carthage. In the Old Testament these versions had been made from the Sep-

tuagint, thus making the Old Latin versions inferior translations. Attempts were made to revise these divergent translations. This presented a serious problem in that none of the
Latin versions received universal acceptance or undisputed
authority.

Jerome felt this situation keenly. Born in 347 A.D. he later
became a monk and a priest. He learned Hebrew and was
familiar with Origen's work. Pope Damasus encouraged
Jerome to undertake a critical revision of the Latin Vulgate.
Jerome's revision of the Old Latin versions was not satisfactory and so in 391 A.D. he embarked upon a new translation
of the Old Testament on the basis of the Hebrew and
Aramaic. After fifteen years of persistent effort he produced
the version known as the Vulgate. It was far superior to the
Old Latin version regarding its accuracy to the original text
and its literary qualities. Jerome's version, however, met
with great opposition in the Western church and his translation was accused of servility to the Jews. His new version
of the Psalter was never adopted.

The Vulgate experienced the same misfortune as did the
Septuagint. Like the latter the Vulgate was disfigured by
numerous alterations, interpolations and errors common to
all copyists of manuscripts, so much so that the text left by
Jerome in the fifth century was considerably altered from
his original version. In the course of the Middle Ages a
number of unsuccessful attempts were made to correct the
Vulgate text and to restore it to its pristine form.

Jewish Biblical Criticism

It is to Jewish students and to the synagogues that Christians are greatly indebted for the preservation of the Old
Testament in the original. Those scholars who took upon
themselves the responsibility of preserving the Hebrew text

36

are known as Massoretes. They were anxious that the corruptions caused by copyists should be kept at a minimum. They also made themselves responsible for supervising the preservation of the Hebrew-Aramaic text.

At the beginning of the Christian era there was only a consonantal text in existence. Those who read the Old Testament Scriptures had to determine for themselves the pronunciation of the words. Different schools of Massoretes, one group in Babylonia, two other groups in Palestine, tried to fix the pronunciation of the text. The pronunciation of the text proposed by the school of Tiberias was finally adopted. The exact date for the adoption of the vocalized text is not known but it was during the eighth and ninth centuries that all manuscripts were supplied with this vowel system.

The Massoretic scholars also developed various types of Massora. The massora consisted of a series of remarks made about the Hebrew text. In a rabbinical Bible the following types of massora are found: the initial, the marginal and the final. In these various massoras, scholars called attention to difficulties and variants as well as the number of letters and words in each book. The Hebrew text as stabilized by the Jews is known as the Massoretic text.

Interpretation as found in the commentaries from the Koran, as well as the rabbinical exegesis found in the Talmud, is not considered critical. Jewish exegetical efforts were primarily concerned with obtaining from the Bible a literal exposition of the legal, religious, historical and ethical teachings of the Bible.

Jewish interpretation is believed to have reached its greatest glory during the Middle Ages with the efforts of Saadia (892–942 A.D.), who translated the Bible into Arabic and interpreted the Old Testament literally. Abraham ibn of Toledo another Jewish scholar also wrote commentaries as did the Jewish interpreter Solomon ben Issac, surnamed Rashi. To the traditional approach Rashi added a new spirit. Concerning his method of interpretation Miss Smally wrote: "Much of his commentary is strictly scientific and rational and in accordance with the spirit of the Hebrew language to which he was finely sensitive. He pays due attention to grammar and syntax, and shows attractive, if rudimentary, appreciation of the principles of comparative philology."[1] While his interpretation is often in conflict with the halacha, he never excluded the latter. Rashi had followers who further developed their master's method. Many Jewish exegetes enthusiastically turned to the most literal interpretation of the Bible. Among these were Rashbam, Eliezer of Beaugency and Joseph Bekhor of Orleans. They had, however, a tendency to explain away the miracles of the Old Testament.

Maimonides, a Jew born in Cordoba in 1135, was more of a philosopher than an exegete. In his famous *Guide for the Perplexed* he commented on the Law. In his interpretative efforts he employed Aristotle's philosophy and thus anticipated the great scholastics who also were to come under Aristotelean influence. Maimonides was mainly interested in the intellectual and social roles of the prophets. With Maimonides the great period of Jewish interpretation came to an end, although the Hebrew exegesis continued in the Middle Ages.

The Christian Middle Ages
During the Middle Ages Christians also studied and interpreted the Bible. Commentaries came into existence that were called *catanae* (chains), in which were placed chosen excerpts of patristic exegesis. During the twelfth century

the Victorines who were particularly influenced by Jewish exegesis studied the Bible on the basis of the original languages. The greatest of these was Andrew of St. Victor. To throw light on Holy Scripture he resorted to the resources of ancient literature, especially Roman writers. His commentaries have foreshadowings of the same interpretation that were to characterize later biblical interpretation.

A number of scholars broke away from the allegorical exegesis of Origen and St. Gregory the Great. During the thirteenth century these scholars were studying Greek and Hebrew, retranslating the Psalter from the Hebrew. Men like Raymond Martini and Nicholas de Lyra were using critical methods and emphasizing the need for literal interpretation. Ideas and methods used by these men were to be later employed as standard approaches by Protestant scholars.

The Renaissance and the Reformation
With the invention of printing a new impetus was given to biblical study. The editors of the first printed Bibles were confronted with manuscripts having divergent readings and this necessitated deciding what readings were to be used.

Some of the great humanists became biblical scholars as was the case with Erasmus. In 1516 Erasmus published his revised Latin translation of the New Testament based on Greek manuscripts. He edited a number of commentaries on the fathers and emended especially the texts of those commentaries that were corrupt. In France Lefevre published biblical commentaries between 1521 and 1524 and also made a French translation of the New Testament and the Psalter.

With Luther there was inaugurated a new era in biblical

studies. The Wittenberg Reformer undertook a hermeneutical revolution without which the Protestant Reformation
could not have been achieved. Luther insisted that the
original languages should be studied and he himself translated the New Testament into German in 1521 and the Old
Testament with the help of co-reformers by 1534. Tyndale
used Luther's September Testament and was influenced by
the German Reformer. Because of Luther's emphasis on
the Word of God as authority in religion, a great deal of
stress was placed upon biblical study. The Bible was considered the only source of faith. Luther's Bible translation
became the inspiration for translations being made in many
of the European countries.

In the sixteenth century the science of textual criticism
was emphasized anew, with the avowed purpose of finding
as pure a text as possible. Thanks to the printing press,
critics could be supplied with the tools for textual criticism,
namely, folio editions of the Hebrew, Greek, Syriac and
Latin texts of the Bible in parallel columns. The following
polyglot Bibles, the Alcala, the Antwerp, Paris and London
published between 1517 and 1653, furnished the necessary
texts for comparison.

The Birth of Modern Biblical Criticism
Many scholars like to mark the beginning of modern biblical criticism with the work of Richard Simon (1638–1662) a
member of the Oratorians. Versatile in Greek, Hebrew,
Syriac and Arabic, he published *A Critical History of the
Old Testament.* In this book Simon questioned parts of the
Pentateuch as originating with Moses. In the second book
of the *Critical History* Simon gave an evaluation of the
various ancient translations and showed the need for textual criticism. In the third book he outlined the princi-

ples the critic must follow when carrying out his critical task. Protestants were criticized for having left the traditions of the Church and thereby were said to have lost the meaning of Scripture. Simon also published a critical history of the New Testament in three volumes. His books were banished by the Catholic Church and attacked by Protestant writers. Present-day Roman Catholic scholarship is in high praise of Simon, claiming that he showed the way in the areas of textual, literary and historical criticism. He is credited with having foreseen most of the problems scholars are grappling with today.

Simon's successor in France was Jean Astruc, court physician of Louis XIV. In 1753 he published a work on the Pentateuch which in the estimation of many scholars marks the true beginning of Pentateuchal criticism. Noticing that in Genesis God was given different names, Astruc proposed to distinguish sources on the basis of the two names of Yahweh and Elohim.

An older contemporary of Richard Simon was Pascal, a philosopher. Belonging to the same generation was Spinoza, a Jewish thinker. Pascal and Spinoza in the *Pensees* and *Tractatus Theologico-politicus*, respectively endeavored to compare philosophical thinking with the Bible. Both Pascal and Spinoza had been influenced by the writings of Descartes. Pascal rejected Descartes as "vague and useless," a position that Spinoza took about the Bible. Spinoza, a pantheist, claimed that Scripture consists of many books, written at different times for different generations of men by different authors. Astruc in 1753 discovered what he supposed to be the double strand of Priestly and Yahwist tradition in the book of Genesis and since that time his approach has been applied to other Old Testament biblical writings.

How Dependable Is the Bible?

While the Old Testament was the first part of Scripture to be subjected to criticism by scholars opposed to direct revelation by God as set forth in the biblical writings, and to the idea of verbal inspiration, the New Testament did not escape the critical approach of the eighteenth century. Reimarus, a rationalist, wrote a work that was circulated secretly and anonymously and that remained unpublished during his lifetime. The dramatist Lessing published the Reimarus manuscript under the title, *On the Purpose of Jesus and His Disciples–One More Fragment by the Anonymous Writer of the Wolfenbüttel* (1778). This work is characterized by a polemic against all forms of supernaturalism. It portrayed Jesus as a mere man. This book propounded all the questions which subsequently would be discussed at length by critical scholars.

According to De Vries, the eighteenth century was said to be "a great century of progress" in biblical studies, and this advancement was associated with the higher critical method. During the eighteenth century, traditional church dogmas are said to have suffered severe shocks from which the church never recovered. Also during this century rationalism became prominent mainly through the efforts of Wolff and Kant who made reason the norm as opposed to the mysteries of faith. The attacks of rationalism touched the very center of the Christian faith.

The dominant philosophy during the first decades of the nineteenth century was the idealistic monistic philosophy of Hegel (1770–1831). Schleiermacher was another philosopher-theologian who subjected Christian doctrine and the Bible to rationalistic interpretation. Schleiermacher dealt with the Gospels in practically the same manner as Reimarus. Under Hegel's and Schleiermacher's influence a number of their followers tried to reconstruct "the historical" Jesus. The most famous or infamous, depending on one's views, was that of David Frederick Strauss (1838). In his book the idea of the so-called "mythical" theory of the Gospel narrative of the life of Christ was proposed. While the position of Strauss was unacceptable to many scholars, yet critical scholars adopted many of his suggestions. Out of his thinking there was formulated the so-called Markan hypothesis by Weiss in 1838 and subsequently the two-document theory of Holtzmann (1863) and of Bernard Weiss (1882).

New Testament criticism during the second half of the nineteenth century followed either Hegelian lines or those of an extreme form of rationalism. Ferdinand Friedrich Bauer applied the Hegelian dialectic to the development of Christianity. Many writers of the life of Christ followed the lines of rationalistic interpretation, the most famous being Ernest Renan's *La Vie de Jesu*, published in 1863. His life of Christ was a caricature of who Christ actually was. Another contemporary of Renan was William Bousset who identified Jesus' kingdom of God with the fatherhood of God and the brotherhood of man. This was more or less the position of Adolph von Harnack in *Das Wesen des Christentums*. Wilhelm Wrede went so far as to state that Jesus never thought of himself as the Messiah (cf. his *Das Messias-geheimnis in den Evangelien*).

In the Old Testament field the nineteenth century saw further developments in higher criticism. J.G. Eichhorn, a Lutheran professor at the University of Jena, has been called "the father of modern higher criticism." He embodied the ideas of Herder and Astruc in his *Introduction to the Old Testament* (three volumes, 1780–83). With him there began the period of the use of the critical method that denied the Mosaic authorship of the Pentateuch and the reconstruction of many books of the Old Testament according to the "scissor and paste method." The period of literary criticism is said to have come to an end with Steuernagel's *Lehrbuch der Einleitung in das Alte Testament.* Until the appearance of Julius Wellhausen, Old Testament efforts had centered on the fragmentizing and dissection of the Old Testament books with much of the historical literature declared mythical and unreliable. For the literary critics the books of the Old Testament contained errors, discrepancies and contradictions.

The concept of the evolutionary development of religion was applied by Wellhausen to the religion of the Old Testament in his *Prolegomena to the History of Israel* (1878). He relied heavily on the writings of Graf and Kuenen. According to Weiser, a current Old Testament scholar, the Graf-Kuenen-Wellhausen views have continued to influence Old Testament studies to the present time.

The use of the historical critical method was opposed by conservative theologians like Hengstenberg, Haevernick, Keil and others because its use produced doubt, skepticism and unbelief. That the historical critical method was a neutral method that did not operate with presuppositions that were hostile to the claims of Scripture is not substantiated by facts.

With the year 1880 there arose a new movement in biblical studies; one that utilized the findings of non-Christian religions and was known as the *religionsgeschichtliche Schule* (School of Comparative Religions). Members of this school began to avail themselves of the abundant light shed by archaeological discoveries in Babylon and Egypt. Proponents of this school endeavored to show the cultural, religious and literary dependence of the

Old Testament on various nations of the Near East. For a time there was a pronounced tendency to trace everything in the Old Testament as coming from Babylon. Advocates of this theory were known as Panbabylonists. This movement was soon rejected by most Old Testament scholars. The school of comparative religion approached the Old and New Testaments from the viewpoint of evolution and dealt with the religion of Israel and the teachings of Christ and the Apostolic Church as religious movements not different in kind, but only in degree, from other religious manifestations of the near eastern world.

Developments in the Twentieth Century

The beginning of the twentieth century witnessed another critical development which was different from the method of literary criticism in use for at least 150 years. This new methodology arose out of dissatisfaction with the results of Old Testament literary criticism. In the new approach, oral tradition became the starting point. Herman Gunkel is usually credited with sponsorship of this new way of dealing with biblical literature. He and his friend Hugo Gressmann were the two outstanding early leaders of this new interpretative methodology who applied form criticism to the Old Testament. Gunkel and Gressmann insisted that the Bible be treated as an ordinary piece of literature. Both men endeavored to show in their earliest writings how foreign influences had operated upon the Old Testament. From a confessional evangelical point of view these men must be classified as opponents to the true biblical religion. The *formgeschichtliche* school was concerned with finding extra-biblical material with the purpose of obtaining a better understanding of the literary genres of the Bible. Gunkel in his *The Israelite Literature* proceeded to outline what he held was a presentation of the Old Testament's development of religious belief. This new approach proposed to examine the origin and development of individual religious ideas and expressions of piety and endeavored to delineate the changes that may have taken place.

Since oral tradition is alleged to have preceded the recording of the first documents J and E, one of the concerns of Old Testament scholars using form criticism was to trace the pre-history of the biblical books or documents where a book is imagined to be a mosaic of different sources. An attempt has been made to determine the supposed changes through which the tradition went as a result of new life situations. The "geology" of the text is an area where scholars can demonstrate their creativity by putting forth interesting theories as to what may have occurred during the time that the tradition or cycles of traditions were being put into written form. Cultic centers, about which not too much is known, in form criticism assume great importance as the creators of traditions and also as places where traditions were supposed to be reformulated or represented.

In a discussion of developments in the field of biblical interpretation in the twentieth century, the method of demythologization must be mentioned. In a new and original manner the concept of myth was applied to the New Testament by Rudolph Bultmann in 1941 in his famous article "The New Testament and Mythology." Bultmann claimed that modern twentieth century man does not believe in miracles and heavenly beings, nor can he accept the whole framework of reference of the christological myth, that is, the belief in a heaven or a hell, the Old and New Aeon and a second return of Christ for judgment. In order not to discard or abandon the Gospels entirely,

Bultmann claims the Gospels must be demythologized. Utilizing an existentialistic understanding of the Christian faith, derived by Bultmann from Kierkegaard and Heidegger, Bultmann claims the Gospels must be interpreted in a completely different way than was traditionally done. The account of the Gospel was not meant to record supernatural events but rather by mythical garb the Gospel was to make man aware of the terribleness of his existence, namely, that he is enslaved to the powers of this world, sin and death. According to Bultmann's understanding of the Gospel narrative, existence is not changed by what Christ did, but purely by *hearing* the Gospel.

Bultmann has had a large group of followers that have developed a system of interpretation, usually referred to as the "new hermeneutic." Most of his followers are form critical scholars. A number of Bultmann's pupils have departed from the position of their master and since the end of World War II have embarked on a new quest for the "historical Jesus," supported by a new form of criticism known as *Redaktionskritik,* redaction criticism. This sometimes is called redaction history. Early form critics disregarded the editorial work of the Synoptic authors in the process of gathering, selecting and setting forth their life of Christ. The post-Bultmannians are attempting to assess the primary source material for the purpose of determining the intention of the Gospels in their present form.

4
Revelation, Inspiration and Biblical Criticism

In this twentieth century the subject of "revelation" has received much attention. Theologians of different religious backgrounds have devoted considerable effort and time during the last four decades to a discussion of revelation in relationship to religion in general and to biblical faith in particular. In discussing the topic of this chapter it will be necessary to distinguish between revelation and inspiration and then to define the twofold aspect of revelation as well as the nature of inspiration and show their relation to biblical criticism.

In both the Old and New Testaments a number of different words are employed to designate the idea of making truths and facts known by God, known to man. In a general sense the different biblical words imply that anything that was not formerly known was called to man's attention. The English word "revelation" comes from the Latin *revelatio* which means unveiling or uncovering. The corresponding word in Greek is *apokalypsis*, the title for the last book of the New Testament.

What is the relationship of revelation to inspiration?

Historically speaking revelation preceded inspiration. In this chapter the term revelation is being employed in a restrictive sense, namely, to designate the unveiling of truths by God which man by himself could not have known. In the evening a moon in the sky is not a matter of revelation but of observation. The truth that God created the universe and the world is a matter of revelation. There are many facts and truths recorded in the Bible that are not matters of revelation but of observation and investigation. Luke the Evangelist relates that he had consulted other accounts of the life of Jesus before he wrote his biography of Christ for Theophilus. The great difference between revelation and inspiration is that the Bible contains a revelation from God and makes known revelatory acts over the centuries, but it is improper to speak of the Bible as containing inspired writings, because all of the books comprising the Bible are inspired by the Spirit of God. Revelation assures men that they have a knowledge of God which He has deigned to give of Himself; inspiration certifies that these revelations given men in written form in the biblical books are truthful and correct. With St. John, the last writer of the New Testament, the giving of new revelations has ceased; simultaneously inspiration has likewise ceased. Since the death of the Apostle John no new revelations have been given to man.

The Bible has demonstrated that a prophet may receive a revelation and yet not understand the significance of what was made known to him. The Old Testament statesman Daniel, to whom Yahweh vouchsafed revelations of the future, did not understand the significance of the visions he received; (cf. Dan. 9:22; 10:12–14); St. John on the Island of Patmos required an angel to interpret the meaning of the visions given him. According to I Pet. 1:10–12 a subsequent

49

revelation was sometimes required to give definiteness and clearness to previous revelations.

On the basis of biblical data students of Scripture have spoken of revelation as being two-fold: in nature and in the Scriptures. We thus possess what is known as a natural and supernatural revelation of God. In recent decades Barth and his followers have argued against a natural revelation, claiming that apart from Christ the revelation in nature could not properly be understood. The first six verses of Psalm 19 declare that God has given a revelation of Himself in nature which is constantly testifying to the Creator. Paul in Rom. 1:19ff. clearly asserts that the heathen are without excuse, "for all that may be known of God by men lies plain before their eyes; indeed God himself has disclosed it to them. His invisible attributes, that is to say his everlasting power and deity, having been visible, ever since the world began, to the eye of reason, in the things he has made" (NEB). Because man is without excuse in that he can know the existence of God and also infer certain attributes of God from a study of nature, man should conform his moral conduct in the light of the revelation that nature has furnished. In his Areopagus address in Athens (Acts 17) Paul, in referring to the monument dedicated to "the unknown God" of the Athenians, described to his audience of Stoic and Epicurean philosophers the known God who provided rain and sunshine and who in the arrangement of changing seasons had made provision for the welfare of His creatures.

Natural revelation is not always understood as it should be because man's mind has become corrupt. The reason for man's apostasy and mental depravity is due to his initial fall from God (Genesis 3). Man made in the image of God became a rebel subject to evil passions and consequently blind to spiritual values. His heart also became subject to corruption (Rom. 3: 10–18; Eph. 2:1ff.). With the fall of man not an evolution but a devolution began so that man finally became so degraded as to worship creeping things" (Rom. 1:23). By his disobedience to God's laws man has become afflicted with a blindness which prevents him from properly understanding God's revelation in nature. The noetic effects of sin have darkened man's mind so that natural revelation which objectively can be seen is often not correctly grasped by man.

The Scriptures teach that natural revelation is universal. At no time in history has God left Himself without witness (Acts 14:17). Natural revelation is universal in scope and territory. God's glory is seen whenever a heavenly body can be observed. Paul told the Athenians that "they should seek God in the hope that they might feel after him and find him yet he is not far from each one of us (Acts 17:27 RSV). Though men may refuse to recognize the revelation that God has placed in nature, it is still there (Ps. 19:1; 104:13, 24). Just as natural revelation was present before man sinned, so it still exists after his fall. Paul teaches that this natural revelation is judicial, a truth emphasized three times by him (Rom. 1:24; 26, 28). Contrary to the light that they had, men "exchanged the truth of God for a lie, and worshiped and served the creature rather than the Creator" (RSV). Natural revelation, however, is insufficient in man's present state; from nature man can never infer the need for a personal Savior; in fact, it is only with a new and regenerated mind that man can properly understand natural revelation.

God has especially revealed Himself in the Bible. God's entire revelation is to be found in the sixty-six books of the Old and New Testaments. Each biblical book is a part of

51

God's supernatural revelation. For Christian churches there has been only one supernatural revelation, that found in the Scriptures.

Central in God's book of revelation, the Bible, is the plan of salvation. This plan conceived before the creation of the universe and the world can never be ascertained from the revelation of God imbedded in nature. God's plan of salvation is unfolded in the individual books of the Bible. The Old Testament makes preparation for the realization of the plan of salvation, while the New Testament tells how through the life and death of His Son this was accomplished. The plan of salvation set forth in the Sacred Scriptures would have been unnecessary if mankind had not fallen into sin. Had Adam and Eve remained in the state of integrity in which they were created, no written revelation of God would have been necessary.

Even though a distinction is made between general and special revelation, God's revelation is nevertheless a unity that must not be severed. Prior to the fall into sin, God had given Adam special oral revelations. He was told to be fruitful and multiply, to eat of all the trees with the exception of one, the tree of knowledge of good and evil. Since man's fall it is insufficient and inadequate for him to rely only on natural revelation. The latter is not to be despised or minimized, but the history of Christian thought has shown that so-called theistic proofs as advocated by natural theologians eventually were not able to withstand a decline into naturalism.

The Bible always correlates general revelation with special revelation. Thus in the prologue to John's Gospel, the Logos (Jesus Christ) is said to be the Creator and Redeemer. Carl Henry observed: "that the Bible does not present general revelation on the thesis that the true knowledge of

God is possible to fallen men through the natural light of reason apart from a revelation of Christ, but rather introduces general revelation alongside special revelation in order to emphasize man's guilt."[1]

Because of man's reliance on reason, many deny and reject the teaching of a supernatural revelation for various reasons. The proponents of different schools of philosophy have presented many perversions relative to God's nature and being, and have advanced erroneous views.

Deism is a philosophical system that has repudiated the traditional biblical belief of supernaturalism. The only revelation that the deists acknowledge is God's revelation in nature. From this basic position the deists denied the concept that God revealed truths, that miracles were employed by God in biblical times or that biblical prophets could predict future events. Eventually the philosophy of English deism spread to France, Holland, Germany, Italy and other European countries where at the same time in the writings of theologians a new system was developed in interpreting the Bible that eventually led to a liberal approach to the Scriptures. The movement known as "higher criticism" may be said to be a direct outgrowth of deism.

Various forms of idealism were also hostile to the biblical concept of special revelation. Plato had proposed the existence of "eternal ideas" which he taught were accessible to men by rational contemplation. In addition, Plato also taught men to disregard history as the arena where meaningful events transpired. These Platonic ideas militated against the biblical teachings which espoused that God initiated and was responsible for particular events in history. The idea of idealism that God's revelation is only general and is accessible to all people is inimical to the biblical

53

teaching that God has given a unique revelation in the Scriptures. It also militates against the biblical view that God has acted through a number of specific successive events that reached their climax in the birth, death and resurrection of Christ.

In the eighteenth century European rationalism reverted to the old Greek idea that historical facts are not absolute but relative, with the result that revelation was separated from historical reality and associated with ideas alone. Christian scholars who adopted this position still professed to believe in Christian revelation but their ambivalence resulted in the separation of special revelation from natural revelation, the former being completely disassociated from historical happenings. This form of rationalism abrogated various aspects of redemptive history. It substituted the distinctive biblical teaching of a special revelation for the idea that revelation is only general and available to all men. This obliterated the distinctive teaching of the Christian faith and meant that there was nothing special or unique about the Virgin Birth, the Atonement and the Resurrection of Christ.

While idealistic philosophies denigrated the historical process, the evolutionary theory that came to prominence in the nineteenth century emphasized anew the importance of historical process. English deism had stressed the transcendence of God, evolution eliminated the concept of transcendence and immanence became the type of revelation that was accepted. The principle of evolution became the ultimate explanation as to the nature of revelation and God was identified with developmental process. The postulation that reality is constantly changing is completely opposed to the idea that the great non-repeatable events of the incarnation and resurrection of Christ are the unique center of redemptive revelation. From a biblical point of view the life of Christ represents the apex of history. The next outstanding historical event will be the return of Christ for the judgment of all nations and men. The past events of biblical history are of no particular importance to the idealist because these happenings are considered a part of the development of history. Neither have the great events in Christ's life any significance for the present or future as is the contention of biblical Christianity.

The Bible teaches that man was made in the image of God and that man at the beginning was created a rational creature with whom God could communicate. Both natural and supernatural revelation would be meaningless unless man had the capability of understanding these revelations. According to evolution mind itself is supposed to have been a late product in the developmental process. In modern philosophy there has been a revolt against reason. Modern philosophy has been skeptical about "the limitations of human knowledge about the spiritual world." The modern revolt is, therefore, opposed to the scriptural position that God has communicated to man truth about Himself and that truths revealed in Scripture are reliable.

Since Schleiermacher, who emphasized the feelings as the seat of authority in religion, there have appeared anti-intellectualistic strands in philosophy and theology. Carl Henry claims that "Schleiermacher's formulas, that we know God only in relation to us and not as He is in Himself, and that God communicates life and not doctrines, have been influential in encouraging an artificial disjunction in many Protestant expositions of special revelation."[2]

Twentieth century neoorthodoxy has sponsored the view

of non-identification of special revelation of God with the Bible. Neoorthodox theologians hold that only Christ should be identified with the Word of God. The Bible in its entirety is said not to be God's word but in many places contains it. Such a view conflicts with the assertions of the Old and New Testaments.

The Biblical Doctrine of Inspiration
The Bible is an authoritative book and has been a power in millions of lives because of its claim to have been inspired by God Himself. Concerning the importance of the biblical teaching of inspiration Wick Broomall has asserted: "There is hardly any subject in the realm of theology which is more crucial than that which relates to the nature of the Bible . . . Back of all the great facts and doctrines of the Bible stands, like a mighty fortress, the supernatural inspiration of the written documents in which these facts and doctrines are recorded."[3] If the books that comprise the Bible are merely of human origin, then it follows that the facts and doctrines found in them are only as reliable as all human knowledge can be. If the Bible is a purely man-made production, then all the limitations adhering to human writings must also characterize the biblical books. Its assertions will be subject to human evaluation and human acceptation or rejection. If the Bible is merely a human book, the declarations and views of the biblical writers can be accepted or rejected in the same manner as assertions by Buddah, Zoroaster, Plato, Aristotle, Kant, Goethe, or Ghandi. "If on the other hand, the biblical records were reproduced by men directed and controlled by the Holy Spirit, then we have every reason to believe that the facts and doctrines recorded in the Bible are free of those imperfections and blemishes that characterize all purely

human productions."[4] Assuming the latter assumption is true, men and women can turn to the Bible with confidence believing that the events and doctrines found in it are trustworthy because they were recorded by God-inspired men.

Down through the ages the Christian Church has been convinced that the Bible in its entirety was "inspired" by God. The word "inspired" needs to be clearly defined because in our day it is used in many different senses. Great and noble art is said to be inspiring. To see the American flag raised on certain occasions can be inspiring. Good music inspires some people. However, the Bible is said to be inspired in a different sense. On the authority of the Bible itself, Christians have believed that the Scriptures were produced or inspired by God. The Bible is God's Word and does not merely contain God's Word.

The classical biblical passage teaching what is involved in the inspiration of the Bible is II Tim. 3:16: "All Scripture is God-breathed" (Greek: theopneustos) which means that God's Spirit caused human writers to record what they did. The word "inspired" is employed in the Revised Standard Version as the translation for the Greek word "theopneustos" which literally means according to the Greek dictionary "God-spirated" or "God-outbreathed." This term definitely affirms that the Old Testament in its entirety is the product of God's breath; in other words, God is its author. The biblical meaning of "inspired" therefore rises above the tendency to define inspiration merely as "dynamic." In former times the term "plenary" was employed together with the term inspiration when describing the nature of the Bible. By plenary inspiration is meant full inspiration. Applied, this term asserts that in toto the Bible was inspired. "Plenary inspiration" also meant that the Scriptures are verbally inspired. Sometimes the phrase "verbal plenary inspiration" is employed by theologians to indicate the unique character of the Bible. This means that God superintended the choice of the very words the human authors used to express facts and truths that they were motivated to write.

The first portion of the Old Testament is associated with Moses who claims to have been a prophet. He calls himself the founder of the prophetic order and depicts himself as the mediator of the priestly teachings and the law. Yahweh told Moses that he was to be His mouthpiece to the people of Israel. According to Deuteronomy 34, possibly written by Joshua, it is stated that never again did there arise a prophet in Israel like Moses whom the Lord knew face to face.

In the Old Testament the prophets in both their speech and writings constantly claim that they were spokesmen for God. They believed that the truths they uttered were those given them by Yahweh, the only true God, in comparison with whom the gods of the surrounding nations were as nothing. The prophets of the Old Testament expected the people to whom they directed their messages not only to accept them as of divine origin, but the people were to obey the contents of these messages. Thus the oft repeated formula: "Thus saith the Lord" occurs more than 2,000 times in the Old Testament. Those persons who do not accept the assertions of the prophets, who claimed to be the recipients of God's message, must logically conclude that these chosen men of God were either deceiving themselves or were frauds.

Most of the New Testament assertions about the divine character of the Scriptures are made about the Old Testament, the Bible of the first Christians. In John 10:34-36

Jesus clearly showed that he considered the entire Old Testament inspired. According to John 10:34 Jesus singled out that "the Scripture cannot be broken." Carl Henry claims that this reference "is doubly significant because it discredits the modern bias against identifying Scripture as the Word of God, on the ground that this assertedly dishonors the supreme revelation of God in the incarnate Christ."[5] However, in John 10:35 while referring to Himself as the One the Father consecrated and sent into the world, Jesus nevertheless alludes to a past dispensation "to whom the Word of God came and the Scripture cannot be broken." The inescapable conclusion is that the whole of Scripture is of irrefutable authority.

This same position was taken by Christ in the Sermon on the Mount when He said: "Think not that I have come to abolish the law and the prophets: I have come not to abolish them but to fulfill them. For truly I say to you, till heaven and earth pass away, not an iota, not a dot, will pass away from the law until it is all accomplished. Whoever then relaxes one of the least of these commandments and teaches men so, shall be called the least in the kingdom of heaven . . . (Matt. 5: 17 ff. RSV). That Jesus considered the Old Testament inspired and dependable is also shown from His frequent statements that events which were going to transpire in connection with His ministry had to be fulfilled as it was written (Matt. 26:31; 26:54; Mark 9:12f.; 14: 19,27; John 13:18; 17:12). Whoever faithfully searches the Gospel narratives in the light of Jesus' attitude toward the Old Testament will have to recognize that the assertion made by the famous church historian Reinhold Seeberg is true: "Jesus Himself describes and employs the Old Testament as an infallible authority."[6]

Paul, the author of thirteen New Testament books, as already indicated in II Tim. 3:15-17, regarded the entire Old Testament as God-inspired. In Rom. 3:2 he did not hesitate to refer to the Old Testament writings as the oracles of God. Paul as a Jew and later as a Christian considered each word of the Hebrew Scriptures as the authentic voice of God.

Peter also had a high regard for the Old Testament. There are at least two significant passages in the two Petrine epistles that support the divine origin of the Old Testament Scriptures. In his Second Epistle Peter wrote: "that the word of prophecy" is more certain than the eyewitness experience of the three disciples that were present at the transfiguration of Jesus. The Old Testament Scriptures are said to have a distinct supernatural quality for "holy men of God spake as they were carried along by the Holy Spirit" (II Pet. 1:21). This assertion clearly implies that the Holy Spirit not only caused the human writers to pen what they did but was also the initiator of their prophetic writings.

Most of the New Testament assertions about the divine character of the Scriptures are made about the Old Testament. However, the Apostles also extended the claim to divine origin in their preaching and writing. On Maunday Thursday Jesus promised His disciples the Holy Spirit, who would guide them into all truth and would bring back to their remembrance the teachings that they had heard when they were with Jesus and also the instructions they had received about their conduct after Christ would leave this earth (John 14:26; 16:13). Peter asserted that he spoke by the Spirit of God (I Pet. 1:12). Paul in a number of his epistles assured the Corinthians that his Gospel was not of men but from God. To the Galatians he wrote: "But I certify to you, brethren, that the Gospel which was preached by me is not man's Gospel. For I did not receive it from men, nor was I taught it, but it came through revelation of Jesus Christ (Gal. 1:11–12). The Thessalonian Christians received Paul's commendation "because, when ye received the Word of God which ye heard of us, ye received it not as the word of men, but as it is in truth, the Word of God, which effectually worketh also in you that believe (I Thess. 2:13). In I Tim. 5:18: "For the scripture saith, Thou shalt not muzzle the ox that treadeth out the corn. And the laborer is worthy of his reward," we have a reference to a passage in Luke's Gospel which Paul places on the same plane with the Old Testament Scriptures (Luke 10:7 quoted in I Tim. 5:18).

It was the position of the ancient church that the Bible as a whole and in every part was the Word of God. This view is known as the "high view" of inspiration. This was the attitude toward the Scriptures that was held in all branches of Christendom till the middle of the last century. Dr. Henry claimed that "the historical evangelical view affirms that alongside the special divine revelation in saving acts, God's disclosure has taken the form also of truths and words. This revelation is communicated in a restricted canon of trustworthy writings, deeding fallen man an authentic exposition of God and His relation with man. Scripture itself is viewed as an integral part of God's redemptive activity, a special form of revelation, a unique mode of divine disclosure."[7]

The idea of verbal inspiration as characterizing the autographs has been rejected by many theologians in the last century. The type of criticism used by the opponents of plenary inspiration was to attack the confidence placed by

How Dependable Is the Bible?

Christians in the Bible's teachings concerning science and history. Critics challenging the reliability of the Bible in the areas of science and history contend that the essentials were still being adhered to by stressing the importance of many biblical statements for doctrine and practice. However, a study of the biblical data submitted by the critics reveals that a distinction is not made between the doctrinal and the historical. The history of the Old Testament is important for understanding the central aspect of revelation. Subsequently biblical critics also surrendered biblical teachings dealing with doctrine and ethics. Since Jesus gave His endorsement to the doctrine of Creation as found in Genesis, and accepted the historicity of the patriarchs, also affirming the Mosaic authorship of the Pentateuch, it wasn't long before the critics only accepted those statements of Christ that were in agreement with their moralistic conception of what constituted religion. Traditional Christianity had held to the infallibility of Jesus. This position was now surrendered by many critics because they found it impossible to subscribe to the teachings of Jesus. The existence of angelic beings was acknowledged by Jesus, and He also warned against Satan and the realm of evil spirits. Jesus claimed to have driven out demons from human beings. He depicted His ministry as a conquest of Satan and cited His exorcism of demons as proof of His supernatural mission. Since Jesus believed such so-called erroneous ideas regarding the spirit world and held views about the Old Testament that the critics rejected, it naturally placed Jesus' knowledge under a cloud and demonstrated to the critics that He had a fallible human nature. Those scholars who espoused an empirical approach to religion and who operated with what was known as a scientific methodology could under no circumstances defend the absolute character of Jesus' teaching.

At one time the doctrine of verbal inspiration was only attacked from without the Church, but today it is considered fashionable for so-called Christian theologians to attack this doctrine. They always caricature verbal inspiration as belief in a mechanical inspiration, called by some a "typewriter" inspiration. The biblical writers are depicted as functioning simply as instruments who in a mechanical manner wrote what was dictated to them. However, no creed of any consequence in the Christian Church has advocated a dictation theory of inspiration. While there have been individual theologians who have defended such a view, the major Christian denominations embracing verbal and plenary inspiration have not accepted a mechanical view. This type of inspiration has always been rejected by those who adhere to the truth that in its entirety the Bible, in its autographs, is the inspired and infallible Word of God.

Implications of the Doctrines of Revelation and Inspiration for Biblical Criticism

The fact that the Bible is verbally inspired by God and a reliable revelation from the Holy Spirit has certain implications for those who practice biblical criticism. One clear implication is the uniqueness of the Bible's content. The stance of the school of comparative religions, which had its origin at the end of the nineteenth century, must be rejected because members of this school grafted the New Testament upon pagan ethnic faiths. The Old Testament was unacceptable to this school because of the Old Testament's exclusivistic attitude toward gods other than Yahweh. The Old Testament does not very well accommodate itself to the support of theological universalism. Some members of the school of comparative religion would derive the teachings of the New Testament from Hellenistic

63

mysticism. The theological views of Paul are alleged to have been taken from the mystery cults of the Roman empire.

Another implication flowing from the doctrines of revelation and inspiration is the unity of the Old and New Testaments; they constitute one inseparable whole. Today the unity of the two Testaments is rejected by most critical scholars who will not allow the New Testament to interpret the Old. Since, as has been shown, the Old and New Testament writings originated in the mind of God, it logically follows that the sixty-six books should be unified as far as content, purpose and scope are concerned. This unity is positively demonstrated between Old Testament prophecy and its fulfillment. There are many predictions of historical events as foretold by Isaiah, Jeremiah and other prophets that were fulfilled. The unity of the two Testaments is also shown by the prediction and fulfillment of Messianic prophecy. The biblical student cannot escape the fact that frequently the New Testament refers to events in Christ's life as the fulfillment of Old Testament prophecies. Christ recognized in the three major divisions of the Hebrew Old Testament, the Law, the Prophets, and the Writings, predictions about His suffering, death, resurrection and glorification (Luke 24: 26ff. and 44ff.). This same awareness is also true of other New Testament writers, such as James (Acts 15:15ff.), Peter (I Pet. 1:10ff.), Paul (Rom. 15:8) and John (I John 3:8).

Another implication flowing from the teachings of biblical revelation and inspiration is the concept that God would not contradict Himself or have statements and assertions recorded that are not true. When the proponents of the Documentary Hypothesis postulate four major sources that are said to be distinguishable by their contradictions and divergent theological views that they set forth, then we are faced with a theory that does not comport with the teaching that God does not lie or reveal untruths. Not only the Books of the Pentateuch but the books of Joshua, Judges, I and II Samuel are portrayed as containing duplicate narratives and presenting contradictory accounts of the same events. In their interpretation of many Old Testament historical books, critical scholars claim the writers invented stories that never occurred, thus confusing and deceiving the unsuspecting reader who does not have the benefit of the insights of the critics. Priests at cultic centers are said to have created stories in the interest of promoting their worship centers. In Deuteronomy, for example, laws are ascribed to Moses that were supposedly given to him by Yahweh, when actually they are of much later origin and were supposedly ascribed to Moses to give them authoritative standing. According to literary criticism Deuteronomy, purporting to deal with Moses' day, actually concerns itself with a religious situation in the seventh century B.C. Such a position amounts to a pious fraud that the Holy Spirit is alleged to have inspired! In the Book of Exodus the Ten Commandments are said to have been written by God Himself and given to Moses. The picture drawn by critical scholarship of the origin of the Decalogue completely rejects the biblical answer.

In the New Testament we have a similar situation. Critical scholars find many discrepancies between the Gospel accounts and assume confusing Christian traditions responsible for them. The fourth Gospel is not the work of John and does not portray an accurate account of that which it reports about Christ. Source criticism, form criticism and redaction criticism, as will be shown, deny the clear assertions of the New Testament which mean that like the Old Testament, the New Testament historical books are unreliable and not dependable.

A rational and authentic doctrine of biblical revelation and inspiration can under no circumstances be harmonized with the idea that God the Holy Spirit has caused men to be given a book that is replete with contradictions and misrepresentation of facts.

5
The Reliability of the Biblical Text

All Protestant versions of the Bible in use for the past four hundred years, whether the King James, the British Revised, the American Standard, the Revised Standard, the New English Bible or any of the modern speech renderings are translations based upon the original languages of the Bible. A knowledge of three languages was necessary for those who translated the Scriptures of both Testaments. Most of the Old Testament was written in Hebrew, a Semitic language; however, half of Daniel (2:4–7:28) was composed in biblical Aramaic, another Semitic language closely related to Hebrew, as well as portions of Ezra (4:8–6; 7:12–26). The New Testament was written in Greek, an Indo-European language. The King James Version, the British Revised, the American Standard, the Revised Standard and the New English Bible are translations that were undertaken by groups of scholars; the Old Testament by specialists in Semitic languages and the New Testament by specialists in classical and Koine Greek.

An important question that comes to the mind of discerning Christians when reading the Scriptures is: How reliable is the original text on which the translations were based? The original books of the Bible, called autographs, are no longer in existence, and therefore cannot be consulted for purposes of verifying the present text. Today we are dependent upon copies that have been made presumably from the original autograph. In endeavoring to understand the text underlying our present English translations which were made from printed texts of the Greek New Testament, we must, therefore, reckon with the fact that the text of Sacred Scriptures was transmitted by copyists who sometimes accidently made mistakes or who occasionally may have deliberately changed the text. What students of the Bible find to be the case with the transmission of scriptural texts is also true regarding the transmission of secular literature where original writings are no longer extant. This situation applies to texts of the classics, the writings of Shakespeare and the ancient literature of many nations.

The fact is that the Scriptures have been transmitted by means of copyists who were susceptible to making mistakes and thus errors and faults were recorded and passed by hand from one manuscript to another. Although the Bible teaches that God inspired the original writers to record what was true, accurate and reliable, God did not guide the hands of copyists. To expect a perfect copy of the text to have been preserved would have required a miracle every time a scribe reproduced a manuscript.

It has been estimated that there are between 250,000 and 300,000 variants in the manuscripts of the New Testament Greek text. In the light of this fact, can anyone assert that we possess a reliable scriptural text? Or how can the biblical student assert the reliability of the New Testament message? When opponents and skeptics of the Bible advance these facts, what shall we say? While it is true that in the surviving manuscripts there are about a quarter of a million variant readings, the impression is given that this constitutes a large number of mistakes. However, this large number of New Testament readings is obtained by counting all variations in all manuscripts, including the papyri, uncials, minuscles and lectionaries. This means, for example, that if one word is misspelled 5,000 different times it is counted as 5,000 mistakes. Actually only one mistake has been made but it has been repeated 5,000 times. This is the method employed in arriving at this large number of mistakes. In comparison with other ancient writings the number of errors seems excessive, but this is because students of the New Testament possess so many more manuscripts in comparison with those of books of antiquity. If we had only a few manuscripts for the New Testament the number of errors would be much smaller. Fortunately, however, the more manuscripts at our disposal, the more likelihood we also have for checking mistakes and hence are in a better position to arrive at a reliable text.

What significance do these variations have for the message as reliable documents upon which the faith of the Christian can be based? To answer this question adequately, it will be helpful to call attention to different types of variations in the present New Testament Greek text.

The great majority of variations within the text deal with readings of no consequence; in fact, many of them are so small that they cannot be represented in translation. Very often words in the Greek manuscripts are spelled differently over a period of years. This is similar to changes in spelling that can be noted by comparing the Authorized Version and the King James Version of today. The Greek language also underwent changes which came to be reflected in the various manuscripts that are now available to the textual critic. Thus there are variations in grammar, changes in the spellings of words introduced by later copyists in accordance with the linguistic standards of their day, or in the order of words, as "the Lord Jesus Christ" instead of "Christ Jesus the Lord." In many cases where differences occur in the Greek manuscripts scholars are able to restore the text. Sometimes, however, the variations are substantial involving whole verses that are not trivial nor unimportant and which cannot easily be disposed of. Most of these longer insertions are suspect by text critical scholars.

For example, the Codex Bezae (fifth century A.D.) has the following reading for Luke 6:5: "On the same day, seeing one working on the sabbath day, he said unto him, Man if you know what you are doing, you are blessed; but if you do not know, you are accursed." No other manuscript or version records this alleged saying of Jesus. Scholars are certain that this verse was not a part of the original Gospel of Luke.

John 7:53–8:11 represents a rather substantial variation with twelve verses of text involved. Most recent New Testament translations do not include this pericope about the adulteress brought to Jesus for condemnation. The American Standard Version has bracketed the verses, indicating doubt that they were a component of the Johannine Gospel. The Revised Standard Version has placed the pericope in a footnote. The reason why recent translators regard this text as dubious is because practically all ancient versions do not have these verses. The only manuscript containing them is the Codex Bezae (fifth century A.D.) which is characterized by a number of peculiar readings. After the fifth century we note that the pericope of the adulteress is only found in late eighth century manuscripts. Those manuscripts including this episode have notes in the margin about its dubiousness. Some manuscripts place these verses at the end of John's Gospel; still others have incorporated them after Luke 21:38. Because of the late occurrence of this pericope, textual critics have omitted from the text the story of Christ's dealing with the adulterous woman.

Another example of variations is the verse found in the King James Version in Acts 8:37: "And Philip said, if thou believest with all thine heart, thou mayest. And he answered and said, I believe that Jesus Christ is the Son of God." These words stress the importance of faith in Christ Jesus, supposedly spoken between Philip the evangelist and the Ethiopian eunuch prior to the latter's baptism. Neither the American Standard Version or the Revised Standard Version has the verse as part of Acts 8. It is found in the Latin Vulgate in the seventh century uncial and a number of cursives but because it does not appear in the ancient Greek manuscripts it has been considered unauthentic.

In the King James Version I John 5:7 reads: "For there are three that bear record in heaven, the Father, the Word, and the Holy Ghost; and these three are one." Of all the Greek manuscripts in existence this verse is only found in two of them. These manuscripts are late and come from the fourteenth and fifteenth centuries. Late Latin manuscripts containing this verse placed it into the two Greek copies. All earlier textual evidence is against this reading.

These are examples of significant variations in our text of today but none of these has any important bearing on the scriptural New Testament text. There is not enough clear evidence to warrant seriously questioning the reliability of the New Testament. Since I John 5:7, Acts 8:37 and John 7:53–8:11 are not found in the early manuscripts, it may legitimately be assumed that they are later additions.

71

However, there are instances where the New Testament scholar is faced with the problem of determining the authenticity of certain readings or verses. A well-known example is the conclusion of Mark 16:9–20. What is the problem concerning these verses found in the King James translation but not included in the American Standard, the British Revised, Revised Standard Version or the New English Bible? The two important fourth century uncials, the Vatican and Sinaitic manuscripts on which we rely for the New Testament do not have this conclusion to Mark's Gospel. Neither does the Old Syriac translation have these verses .

In favor of Mark 16:9–20, there are the Alexandrian manuscript, Codex Bezae and other early manuscripts, all late uncials and cursives, five Old Latin authorities, in addition to the Vulgate, one Syriac manuscript, one Old Syriac, the Peshitta version and many other versions. The aforementioned evidence constitutes the negative and the positive positions on this text. Both J. W. McGarvey and Bishop Burton defend the authenticity of Mark 16:9–20, while those scholars rejecting this text base their decision on the reliability of the Vatican and Sinaitic manuscripts.

If the proponents who advocate the rejection of the Markan ending were correct, it would not affect any doctrine or teachings concerning Christ's resurrection. The main events cited in Mark 16:9–20 are recorded elsewhere. Except in a few rare instances we have a reliable New Testament text and one that can be accepted without doubt. In commenting on the question of the reliability of the New Testament text, Prof. F. F. Bruce has written:

In view of the inevitable accumulation of such errors over so many centuries, it may be thought that the original texts of the New Testament documents have been corrupted beyond restoration.

Some writers, indeed, insist on the likelihood of this to such a degree that one sometimes suspects they would be glad if it were so. But they are mistaken. There is no body of ancient literature in the world which enjoys such a wealth of good textual attestation as the New Testament.[1]

Sir Frederick Kenyon, a former great authority in the field of textual criticism of the Bible asserted:

It is reassuring at the end to find that the general result of all these discoveries and all this study is to strengthen the proof of the authenticity of the Scriptures, and our convictions that we have in our hands in substantial integrity, the veritable Word of God . . . The interval then between the dates of original composition and the earliest extant evidence becomes so small as to be in fact negligible and the last foundation for any doubt that the Scriptures have come down to us substantially as they were written has now been removed. Both the *authenticity* and the general *integrity* of the books of the New Testament may be regarded as finally established.[2]

The Text of the Old Testament

Old Testament textual data is not as extensive as that for the New Textament. The principles followed for the restoration of the New Testament are those also applied to the remaining Hebrew manuscripts of the Old Testament. The earliest complete manuscripts are the Cairo Codex of the Former and Latter Prophets dated around 895 A.D. The Leningrad Codex of the Prophets is a little later, dated as coming from 916 A.D. The oldest complete manuscript of the Old Testament is the Leningrad Codex which was completed in 1008 A.D. Many other manuscripts are in existence but these are the basic witnesses to the Hebrew text of the Old Testament. The latest edition of the *Biblia Hebraica* is based on these four manuscripts, particularly the Leningrad Codex.

Why is it that at the present time we only have complete

manuscripts which are between 1500 to 2400 years removed from the Hebrew originals? There are two reasons for the paucity of Hebrew manuscripts as compared with the plethora of existing New Testament Greek manuscripts: one, the Jews were subjected to periodic persecutions during which attempts were made to eradicate their religious books; and second, the custom of the Jews to bury used and defective biblical synagogue manuscripts or scrolls. The Jews reverenced their Scripture with almost superstitious respect which caused them to give ceremonial burial to any defective copies.

Until the age of printing in the fifteenth century, the Hebrew text in the manuscripts was transmitted by hand copying. This mode of transmitting often resulted in scribal errors and mistakes. Not a few letters of the Aramaic square characters which supplanted the use of the Old Phoenecian characters in which Hebrew documents were written, could easily be confused. An example of this would be the well-known name of Nebuchadrezzar, a form which technically is more correct than the form often found in the present Hebrew Bibles as Nebuchednezzar. The difference between the two spellings is found in the mix-up between n (נ) and r (ר) which have similar forms in Hebrew.

After the return to Jerusalem of the children of Israel from their Babylonian captivity there came into existence a class of men known as "scribes" who dedicated themselves to the transmission and preservation of the Hebrew text. They in turn were followed by the scholars of the Talmudic era, placed between 150–500 A.D. These Talmudic scholars continued the efforts of the scribes and endeavored faithfully to hand down the text as received by them.

The scholars that made special contributions to the transmission and preservation of the Hebrew text were the scribes living at Tiberias, known as Massoretes. There was another major school in Palestine and one in Babylonia but the efforts of the Tiberian School seem to have been preferred and perpetuated by future generations. The work of the Massoretes extended from the fifth to the tenth century A.D. The massorete scholars consulted the traditions of the past (massorah) and also made studies about the text which they incorporated in various "massorahs," designated as the initial, marginal and final. The efforts of the Massoretes are best known for the system of vowels and accents which they invented for the consonantal text of the Old Testament which was written without vowels. This practice of omitting vowels still prevails in modern Arabic and Hebrew. When the Hebrew language was no longer spoken, there was the danger that the consonants would not be read correctly which would lead to misinterpretation. Although the Massoretes supplied the vowels for the text, they did not change any of the consonants.

In order to prevent scribal errors in the copying of manuscripts, the Massoretes devised intricate ways of counting the letters of a page by numbering the verses, words and letters of each book. They made all manner of statistical studies about the text designed to transmit an accurate text to future generations. With these safeguards a scribe could check what he had copied against the known facts recorded in the various "massorahs" that had been created. The Massoretes were textual critics who set down what they considered to be the most authentic biblical text. It is this text that we use today known as the "Massoretic text."

The Hebrew manuscripts are the most important course for establishing a reliable text of the Old Testament. They are basic for the science of Old Testament textual criticism.

However, there are some additional sources which have proven useful in a number of ways for textual critics, such as, translations in Greek, Syriac, and Latin made directly from the Hebrew text and known respectively as the Septuagint (Greek), the Peshitta (Syriac) and the Vulgate (Latin). These three primary translations originated between the years of about 250 B.C. to 405 A.D. and are valuable as witnesses to the type of Hebrew text that was available before the age of the Massoretes.

The fact that our earliest Hebrew manuscripts date back no further than the ninth century might cause anxiety about the possibility of having an authentic text with so many hundreds of years intervening between the autographs and our most complete Hebrew manuscripts. However, it helps to allay our fears when we learn that before the time of the Massoretes, Jewish scholars were extremely conscientious, endeavoring to obtain perfection in the transcription of the text. Proof for this position may be found in the Talmud (Jewish civil and religious law) where strict rules were laid down for the preparation of copies of the five books of Moses.

The Massoretes no doubt found variations in the manuscripts received from previous generations, but they took meticulous precautions to detect errors and note them as well as to suggest corrected readings. The Massoretic text undoubtedly goes back to pre-Christian times.

The Dead Sea Scrolls, found since March 1948 have shown that the Massoretic text was already known in the second century before Christ. About 400 rolls, most of them fragmentary, have been found in various Qumran caves. These rolls were produced by a religious community some scholars have identified as the Essenes or a group of people having similar religious tenets. Most of the manuscripts are biblical books and have proven to be of great significance for textual criticism. All biblical books, except Esther, have been found among the scrolls coming from eleven different caves near Khirbet Qumran. Most important among the Qumran manuscripts are the two Isaiah scrolls, designated as Isaiah A, nearly complete, and Isaiah B, containing a considerable portion of the book (chapters 41–59). Isaiah A comes from 100 B.C. or earlier, while Isaiah B is dated somewhat later. As a result of this important discovery, biblical students of the Hebrew Old Testament now have manuscripts that are a thousand years earlier than previous Hebrew manuscripts.

A comparison of these new documents with the medieval Hebrew manuscripts reveals the significant fact that there has scarcely been a change in the Hebrew text in the process of transmission. In evaluating the new Qumran evidence, Professor Bruce wrote: "The new evidence confirms what we had already good reason to believe—that the Jewish scribes of the early Christian centuries copied and recopied the text of the Hebrew Bible with the utmost fidelity."[3]

The Isaiah A scroll was discovered in time to be utilized by the Old Testament committee that translated the Revised Standard Version. From the Isaiah A scroll the RSV adopted thirteen readings which can be recognized by the reference "one ancient manuscript" in the footnotes. Later Dr. Burrows wrote that eight of these adopted readings would not have had to be adopted. However, a number of the adoptions from the Qumran Isaiah appear to be a distinct improvement. A good example is found in Isaiah 21:8 where in the King James it reads: "And he cried: A lion." The Revised Standard Version reads: "He who saw cried," a rendering made possible by using

77

the Isaiah manuscript. The two Hebrew words underlying the King James and Revised Standard translations are quite similar and could be easily confused. The context of the Revised Standard Version makes better sense than that reading in the Authorized Version.

In general, the text of these ancient biblical manuscripts is similar to the Massoretic text. Most of the differences between the Qumran Scrolls and the printed text of the *Biblia Hebraica* are trivial and merely involve spelling differences. This has moved Professor Burrows to assert: "It is a matter for wonder that through something like a thousand years the text underwent so little alteration. As I said in my first article on the scroll, 'herein lies its chief importance, supporting the fidelity of the Massoretic tradition.'"[4]

Christianity as a reliable religion is dependent upon an infallible and inspired biblical text. Some critics claim that biblical readers do not possess such a text. They assert that it has become hopelessly corrupted. While the science of textual criticism purports to be an objective science, textual criticism allows for a certain amount of subjective opinion. Textual critics are influenced by theological presuppositions which affect their judgment as to what degree at present we have a reliable text.

Those Christians who believe the statements of the Sacred Scriptures have been given the assurance that God would not permit His Word to become corrupt. In John 8:31–32 Christ promised: "If ye continue in my word, then are ye my disciples indeed; and ye shall know the truth, and the truth shall make you free." Since Christ admonished people to continue in His Word, He thereby guaranteed them a good and reliable text. Also when Jesus in His high priestly prayer prayed "for them also which shall believe on me through their word" namely, the word of the Apostles, He thereby assured the Church that it will continue to possess a reliable text. It is difficult to believe that if God has given mankind an inscripturated revelation (the Bible) that He would permit His words to become corrupt that future readers of it would be uncertain of its true meaning. Both Old and New Testament textual criticism has reached a point where Christians may believe that in all essentials they have a reliable text.

Christians can be certain that God would not have permitted His Word to become corrupt. Dr. Francis Pieper was right when he averred: "What the Church lacks in our day is not a reliable text of the Bible, but faith in the sufficiently reliable text."[5]

6
How "Historical" Is Old Testament History?

Before the development of that phase of critical movement generally known as Pentateuchal criticism, Christian and Jewish scholars regarded the five books of Moses, Joshua, Judges, I and II Samuel, I and II Kings, I and II Chronicles, Ezra, Nehemiah and Esther as books belonging to the historical literature of the Bible. These books deal with historical events that begin at creation and terminate with the return of the Jews to Judea after the Babylonian captivity. The Old Testament reveals the nation of Israel as a people greatly interested in its past history.

Until the nineteenth century, Christians and Jews had accepted Adam, Noah, Abraham, Isaac, Jacob, Aaron, Moses, Joshua, the individual judges, Eli, Samuel, Saul, David, Ishbaal, David, Solomon, Elijah and other persons discussed and alluded to in the books of Kings, Chronicles, Ezra, Nehemiah and Esther as historical personalities, as well as the events and sayings ascribed to them.

However, this position has changed with the introduction and adoption of literary critical theories regarding the Pentateuch, the Former Prophets and other biblical documents as they came under the scrutiny of critical scholars who often were skeptical in their attitude toward the Bible. With the rejection of the Mosaic authorship there also occurred the questioning of the historicity and facticity of the narratives of many other Old Testament books. Concomitant with the ultimate distribution of the books of the Hexateuch (Pentateuch and Joshua) among the sources J, E, D and P, the historical data of at least eight biblical books were questioned by critical scholars. Anton Hartmann placed the substantial origin of the Pentateuch between the Solomonic era (971–931 B.C.) and the Exile (587 B.C.). He viewed the Pentateuchal narratives as myths and legends. Julius Wellhausen was responsible for the popularization and finalizing of "The documentary hypothesis." A reading of his *Prolegomena to the History of Ancient Israel* shows that he rejected the historical character of many books of the Old Testament and that he placed the order of the historical events in the Pentateuch in reverse of their occurrence. The prophets preceded the priests. He assumed that much of the material that was found in the alleged documents J, E, D and P had been invented by the writers or redactors of these various documents.

In endeavoring to assess the implications of the documentary hypothesis for the understanding of the first five books of the Old Testament, Merrill Unger wrote:

If one maintains that "the contents of the Pentateuch . . . were not first transmitted as a book but as a tradition" and not reduced to writing till centuries after Moses, and then only as two often divergent traditions (J and E) were united with still later Deuteronomic and Priestly additions, the admission is inevitable that the account of the "Mosaic" age set forth in the Pentateuch is fundamentally unreliable. No theory that the later redactors who combined the documents J, E, D and P were "inspired" can alleviate the suspicion of historical unreliability, as such a theory is

81

at variance with the internal evidence of the documents themselves, which ascribe at least two of the three legal codes and considerable narrative directly to Moses' pen.[1]

During the second half of the nineteenth century many scholars took the view that the authors of the J, E, D, P documents reflected in them their own views as to how the history of Israel is supposed to have developed. According to these scholars these documents were more important for shedding light on the time of the authors or editors of these documents than on the earlier periods with which they purported to deal.

Toward the end of the nineteenth century Gunkel became dissatisfied with Wellhausen's conclusions which had conquered the scholarly world and whose writings translated into English exerted in time a great influence in England, Scotland and America. Gunkel believed that in the Old Testament there was material that went beyond the date of the ninth century B.C., the date originally accepted for the oldest document of the Pentateuch. Gunkel claimed that there was a long oral tradition behind these written documents which had changed considerably in the course of transmission. He assumed that the oral tradition was composed of an amalgamation of different types of literary genre. For Gunkel it was necessary to try to determine the *situation in life (Sitz-im-Leben)* that gave birth to the various kinds of literary genre which he isolated. Furthermore, Gunkel held that during the century-long transmission of the oral traditions new *situations in life* developed and resulted in the reshaping of the oral tradition. Thus before the interpreter can deal with a given Old Testament text, it is necessary for him to practice what might be called the "geology of the text" and to establish how the transmission has changed and the nature of the situation that gave birth to the original material. Form criticism—in German: Formgeschichte—as developed by Gunkel, Gressmann and their followers has continued the attack upon the historicity and reliability of many Old Testament books, sections of books and individual chapters of books under the guise of finding in them such literary genre as "myth," "saga," "folk-tale," and "legend."

The insistence of a long period of oral transmission before the main traditions were written and later combined into cycles is a naturalistic device to explain the miraculous in the Scriptures as popular legend and folklore. Supernatural facts, which stand irrefutable and unshaken in the Mosaic documents, impregnable to all other methods of attack, are dissolved like wax in the crucible of the critics by a method purposely invented to reject the miraculous elements.

Modern Conception of Old Testament Historiography

Articles and books written by critical scholars dealing with Old Testament historiography have accepted the presuppositions and the conclusions of form criticism. McKenzie in his *Dictionary of the Bible* sets forth views in an article "History, historical writing" which reject the position formerly held by Jewish, Roman Catholic and Protestant scholars regarding the historical character of large portions of Old Testament books, and he presents a completely different understanding of the concept of history in the Old Testament.

In what sense may we speak of the Old Testament as containing history and historical data? It is the contention of critical scholars that history in the modern sense is not found in the earlier books of the Bible. Thus McKenzie asserts that "in the Bible the narrative passages come from a period and a civilization in which history in the modern sense of the world was entirely unknown."[2] Although there are different conceptions among historians as to what constitutes history, it is claimed that none of the modern understandings of history are found in the Old Testament. To cite McKenzie again: "The modern concept of 'historical fact,' a historical event certainly established as occurring in a definite place and time, was therefore not within the scope of the ancient historian; neither therefore is the correlative concept of 'historical error,' an event of which historical reality is falsely affirmed."[3] In the ancient world it is claimed that history was merely conceived of as "the remembered past." Before the modern understanding of history, the ancients, it is claimed, failed to distinguish between what was told (saga) from what "actually happened" (history). The remembered past could be told either in the form of oral tradition or in written records. McKenzie and those who share his approach to the Old Testament aver that no single book or passage in the Old Testament depicts the past in a manner the modern historian would consider "historical." The memory of past events is imperfectly and incompletely reflected in the biblical historical documents.

Modern Old Testament scholars believe that the Jews, like other ancient peoples, did not know what was involved in writing history nor did they have critical means for ascertaining historical facts. Many Old Testament scholars thus contend that society was not interested in the detailed accuracy of historical knowledge, but in seeing itself as it was. As in the portrait of a person, it was not important that details were accurately pictured but that the portrait captured and rendered visible the genuine personality of the subject. McKenzie claims that in ancient history, as in painting, this could not be done without distortion, exaggeration and omission; but this is the "historical" fact which was the object of ancient history. Only this type of "historical" truth was obtainable for the ancients. Professor North maintains that a distinction must be made between "fact and event." In dealing with the Old Testament, critics contend that it is difficult to ascertain how much is fact or interpretation. To illustrate, North cites the Exodus from Egypt. The various sources (J, E, D, P) give conflicting information as to what actually transpired. That the Hebrews escaped from Egypt and crossed the Sea of Reeds can be considered factual. When, however, the Hebrews say that God delivered them, this is an interpretation; in other words, *Heilsgeschichte* (salvation history) must be distinguished from *Geschichte* (history). Professor North states that conservative scholars and critical scholars differ as to what constitutes history in the Old Testament. Concerning the conservatives he wrote: "The former believe, often passionately, that every Bible narrative or statement is 'fact' in the sense that things happened as exactly described. They make no distinction between event and fact as they have been defined here. *Geschichte* is *Heilsgeschichte* and *Heilsgeschichte* is *Geschichte*."[4] How much of the Old Testament can be classified as *Geschichte* is a matter of dispute.

On the basis of form critical studies, McKenzie, Koch, North, Von Rad and others assume that behind the written documents lies oral tradition. McKenzie warns that as "preliminary we should note that the original form, when it is incorporated into a larger composition, does not have precisely the same meaning which it had when it existed independently. The forms, however, are often discernible in the existing literary complexes. Modern scholars are largely agreed that the forms which occur in writing were shaped in oral tradition long before they were committed to writing."[5]

The form critical school claims that to appreciate the various oral literary forms it must be remembered that storytellers played an important role in determining the oral traditions behind the written documents. It is assumed on the basis of the study of the folk literature of the Greeks and of modern Slavic peoples that there existed professional raconteurs who went from village to village reciting poems and epics. The same practice is ascribed to Israelite raconteurs. However, the existence of such oral storytellers in Israel is based on analogy which is of dubious merit.

The storyteller, it is said, was a master of his material and not necessarily bound by it. As he related the remembered history of his society he made changes as he held dialogue with his contemporaries, and as a creative artist felt free to add, delete, alter and interpret. Thus it becomes obvious that the final textual version may be considerably different from the original situation described in the biblical material. The result of such assumptions is to make the historical books replete with misinformation and errors and thus untrustworthy. This would make the Bible an unclear book and make it impossible for the theologically untrained person to correctly understand much material in the Old Testament.

Critical scholars recognize differences between history, genealogy, legend, saga, myth, covenant-command, legal statement, priestly instruction, and romance. Legend, myth and saga are literary forms that were formerly not believed to exist in the Old Testament, but are now found there by critical scholarship. These three forms of literary genre are not characterized by the recording of facts as they happened or description of events as they did occur.

The saga is supposed to take cognizance of time and place and deals especially with tribes. In the Old Testament we are said to have "sagas" involving Moses, Joshua, the Judges, David and the lives of the patriarchs. Yet another literary form, the "legend" is said to be characterized by a religious interest and concentrates on sacred places and religious rites. Thus the accounts of the origin of circumcision, the Passover, various sanctuaries and stories about the prophets are legendary in character. "The romance," (Ruth) another literary form is said to be an extended narrative and serves often as a medium of entertainment.

Thus many scholars who have adopted the form critical approach to the Old Testament are regarding Old Testament history in a different manner from which it was considered formerly. Critical scholars claim that the manner in which Old Testament writers used their materials would indicate that their purpose was religio-pragmatic. According to C. Epping, a Dutch Roman Catholic scholar, the literature of the Old Testament contains homiletic and didactic tendencies which necessarily resulted in the manipulation of the data. Thus Epping wrote, regarding the "Former Prophets": "Their purpose was not so much to give future generations precise information on what happened in the past, . . . but rather to make the religious elements in the history of the past serve for the instruction of present generations."[6]

[6]From *Encyclopedic Dictionary of the Bible* ed. by Louis F. Hartmann. Copyright 1963, Louis F. Hartmann. Used with permission of McGraw-Hill Book Company.

How Dependable Is the Bible?

The Interpretation of Genesis
According to Form Criticism

The attack by form critics began with Genesis, the fountainhead of divine revelation. Gunkel and Gressmann initiated the attack on the historicity and reliability of this foundational book. Both of these men were rationalists who rejected the uniqueness of the Judaeo-Christian faith. The supernatural element interwoven within the web of biblical narratives, was rejected on a priori grounds. Gunkel's 1901 *Commentary on Genesis* has become the subsequent fountainhead for interpretation by many scholars who reject the historicity and facticity of the narratives of Genesis. In this commentary Gunkel distinguished between history and "Sagen," rendered as "legend" by Carruth the translator of his *Die Sagen der Genesis* (*The Legends of Genesis*). According to Gunkel there is no true history in Genesis. He contended it was erroneous to believe that Genesis contains any kind of material the modern historian would label "historical." One of the criteria employed by Gunkel to identify legend was the presence of the supernatural or miraculous in an episode. The validity of this criterion would remove from serious consideration as ever having occurred at least eighty episodes that contain the miraculous in the Old Testament. Gunkel claimed that legend is the form of literature employed by those who either are not qualified to write history or are not interested in doing so. Legends are supposed to concern themselves with family matters of a more personal nature, are simple in scope and of less "grand" significance.

Another criterion used by Gunkel to distinguish between legend and history was that legend was originally handed down orally while history is usually found in written form.

Writing down historical facts also has the advantage of fixing the data, while legend usually transmitted orally is subject to changes. Legend is therefore said to be an inadequate vehicle for history. While many twentieth century scholars have not accepted all of Gunkel's conclusions regarding the type of materials in Genesis, they have more or less followed his conclusions regarding the type of materials of which the Book of Genesis is comprised. Wellhausen had rejected many books and large portions of the Old Testament as non-historical and non-factual and had depicted the documents J, E, D and P as containing fictional data which no historian could concede as historical. While Gunkel disagreed with some of Wellhausen's basic assumptions, he did aid and abet the idea of the non-historical and non-factual character of many, if not most, of the episodes presented in the Pentateuch and early historical books from Joshua to II Samuel 8.

Present day critics are agreed that Genesis 1–11 constitute a special literary genre, that the narratives in these chapters dealing with the creation of the world, the creation of Adam and Eve, the institution of marriage, the temptation and fall in Eden, the first fratricide, the flood story, the building of the ark by Noah and his three sons, the exit from the ark, Noah's planting of a vineyard, the building of the tower of Babel, the confusion of tongues and the distribution of peoples as set forth in the first eleven chapters, are legendary. Critics claim that these stories called "etiological legends" were invented to explain problems with which early Hebrew man had to grapple. Thus Claus Westermann in *A Thousand Years and A Day* asserted: "The first chapters of Genesis were never intended to do what is in fact, impossible for them; namely, give a historical or scientific description of the origin of the world and the human race. They

89

are the product of a confession—that God is creator of the world and Lord of history."[7] *The New Catholic Encyclopedia* has an article on "etiology" which follows Gunkel's interpretation of this matter in the Old Testament. The etiological origins of many episodes in the Pentateuch, Joshua, Judges, Esther and I and II Chronicles are adopted by various Roman Catholic, Protestant and Jewish writers. Gunkel distinguished between the legends of Genesis 1-11 and those of chapters 12-50, the latter chapters containing legends dealing with the patriarchs of Israel. In these legends, Abraham, Isaac, Jacob and his sons, their locality and sphere of influence, Canaan and the nearby lands, are depicted. Gunkel did not recognize the patriarchs as individuals and denied that in chapters 12-50 we have a reliable account concerning the experiences of Abraham, Isaac, Jacob and Joseph.

While a difference is supposed to exist between Genesis 1-11 and 12-50, according to critical scholars, the resulting interpretations given the latter chapters do not fare much better when evaluated in the light of the question: "To what extent and degree are chapters 12-50 reliable in the type of information they furnish?" Dr. Hooke finds Genesis 12-50 contains "saga." For him the essential difference between "saga" and "myth" is that saga has no connection with ritual and does not necessarily have any religious significance, although "sagas" may be employed to teach religious lessons. In the opinion of Hooke the patriarchal narratives are a mixture of fact and fiction, and a substratum of historical facts underlie the patriarchal narratives of Genesis; but he contends that to distinguish the substratum from the legendary accretions at the present time is impossible. The patriarchs are not individuals but are conceived of as ancestors of tribes; in some instances the characteristics and the history of tribes are reflected in the biography of the ancestors. Frequently, the patriarchs are depicted as the founders of sanctuaries, and legendary explanations were invented to account for the names and customs of these sanctuaries. Sometimes the patriarchs are types of characters and in connections with these characterizations, it is claimed, there developed an idealization of these men designed to serve as patterns of piety and virtue.

The Life of Moses According to Form Criticism

When scholars who have adopted the critical approach to the Old Testament deal with the life of Moses as recorded in the books of Exodus through Deuteronomy, the same manner of handling biblical data is in evidence. Gressmann, an associate of Gunkel, stands out especially in this approach. He postulated a long oral tradition behind the documents that became the foundation for the Documentary Hypothesis. The life of Moses as allegedly set forth by the final redactor or redactors around 400 B.C. was based on four sources, using four different traditions which were often contradictory. Professor McNeile in his discussion of the life of Moses wrote: "While the denial that Moses was a real person is scarcely within bounds of sober criticism, it does not follow that all the details related of him are literally true to history."[8] Many Old Testament critical scholars believe that the books of Exodus, Numbers and Deuteronomy contain a nucleus of facts relative to the life of Moses, yet because of the use of four different traditions many items recorded about Moses need to be questioned and rejected. The miracles intertwined in the life of Moses are categorically rejected or reinterpreted as to practically explain away the literal meaning of the accounts. It is contended that later editors ascribed happenings and sayings which never occurred. Roessler in his article on "Moses" in *The New Catholic Encyclopedia* maintains that little can be known with certainty about Moses because of the transmission of different oral traditions and their use by authors and editors of oral traditions. In Roessler's judgment the miracles are suspect. An article on the life of Moses in the famous German encyclopedia *Religion in Geschichte und Gegenwart* states that it is difficult to deal with the materials in Exodus relative to Moses' life according to the traditionsgeschichtliche methodology.

In Exodus it is claimed different complexes of material have been put together out of individual stories which in themselves bear the characteristics of saga. The Exodus tradition, it is claimed, as found in Ex. 1:1–15: 21, in its present form is determined by the institution of the Passover festival, while the deliverance at the Sea of Reeds presents the scope of the entire account. The German scholars Noth, von Rad and Koch distinguish between the Exodus tradition and the Sinai tradition in the history of Israel, and they have concluded that Moses played a very insignificant role in the history of Israel. Professor Noth, who found in the Pentateuch five different thematic cycles, believed that Moses originally had no part in the Exodus and Sinai tradition complexes and under no circumstances is Moses to be considered the deliverer of the Hebrew nation. If the conclusions of these critical scholars are correct, it would be better to place into the hands of readers von Rad's essay, *Das Formgeschichtliche Problem des Hexateuch* (The Form Critical Problem of the Hexateuch) than to read the so-called garbled and faulty versions of the history of Israel in the biblical books which St. Paul in II Timothy described as God-breathed! To read and understand properly the Pentateuchal narratives, critical scholars maintain that it is imperative to know the existence of a number of conflicting traditions in the biblical books which therefore require the historian to question and reject some data resulting in a reconstruction much different from what the biblical text presents.

Form Criticism and Other Historical Books

According to the proponents of the form critical method, the books of the Hebrew Old Testament called "the Former Prophets," namely, Joshua, Judges, I and II Samuel, I and II Kings contain many legends and mythical material. The historical picture formerly assumed to exist, it is claimed, needs to be revised in the light of the new insights which the form critical method has given us of personalities and happenings. Events in the Book of Joshua have been rejected as unreliable. Dr. Strange, following Noth in *The New Catholic Encyclopedia* states that the episodes in chapters 1–12 are in epic or saga form. This means that the entire conquest of Canaan ascribed to Joshua by the author of the book is actually an idealized account of what was supposed to have occurred. Noth believes that chapters 2–9 contain etiolgies that describe a picture of the Israelite invasion and conquest when these events were shadows and vague in Israel's memory and therefore cannot be accepted. The tribal lists in Joshua 13–22 are of value for the geography of Palestine in the days of David but do not reflect a correct description of Joshua's time.

The Book of Judges does not fare much better at the hands of critical scholars. The credibility of Judges is doubted because of the presence of etiological materials. Various traditions about certain heroes are alleged to have circulated at different cultic centers in Palestine. The Book of Judges, it is averred, has two different contradictory introductions and is a composite book that reflects the record of happenings which never occurred as depicted.

The personality of Samuel is evaluated in a manner similar to that of Moses since, it is claimed, no single sacred institution of Israel, e.g. the offices of prophets, seer, judge or sacrifical intercessor, can be used to characterize Samuel's position. Various segments of the narrative are supposed to evince different interests depending upon which cultic centers they came from. Neither can the narratives of Samuel be accepted as historical but only as theologically interested history according to James Barr. Critical scholars find at least two contradictory sources in I Samuel.

Formerly biblical books like Esther, Ruth, Jonah, Daniel were considered to be writings that reflected accurate historical events. Ruth was a story which told how eventually Obed was born, the grandfather of David. The book of Jonah related how God sent the prophet Jonah to Nineveh, how he tried to escape but eventually did preach that unless the city repented it would be destroyed, and Jonah's unhappiness that the city was spared. According to the new literary criticism, both the books of Ruth and Jonah are said to have been written in the fifth century to counteract the warped position of Nehemiah and Ezra who forbade mixed marriages. Ruth and Jonah are said to represent a different attitude toward foreign people than that exhibited by the Books of Ezra and Nehemiah. The book of Esther is considered fictional in character by the critics, created by a second century writer to account for the celebration of the Purim Feast and as such does not give the true historical occasion for the origin of this festival.

The Book of Daniel, whose first six chapters give historical data, is rejected as coming from the sixth century and Daniel is not considered its author. The purpose of the book is propagandistic in nature, the first of many apocalypses, designed to encourage the second century B.C. Jews to resist the hellenization program of Antiochus Epiphanes.

The last two books of the Old Testament in the Hebrew Bible are I and II Chronicles which have parallel accounts in I and II Samuel and I and II Kings. Because there are accounts in the Books of Chronicles not found in Samuel and Kings, the historicity and reliability of I and II Chronicles have been questioned. In the opinion of many critical scholars the Books of Chronicles are unreliable and the critics have even gone so far as to claim that the author did not report what actually occurred but what should have happened.

Old Testament History is Reliable and Trustworthy
The critical interpretation of Old Testament history, amounting to rejection or reinterpretation as previously indicated, is influenced by the greater questions of whether or not one believes in miracles and predictive prophecy. Without the supernatural strand, Old Testament history would not be Old Testament history at all. It is as Kline has so correctly stated: "Consequently, even if enough evidence were available from archaeology and related sciences to vouch for all the ordinary data (chronological, political, etc.), the history in the Old Testament would still appear radically distorted to those who regard the idea of divine intervention in human affairs as nonsense. Similarly the *view* of history embedded in the Old Testament is not the sort of thing archaeology is able to verify. The Old Testa-

ment's interpretation of the movement of history will call forth agreement according to the reader's total life and world view."[9]

One of the basic assumptions of current biblical criticism which archaeology does not support is that ages of oral tradition had to precede the writing down of the experiences of the Hebrew nation's patriarchs and the record of the founding of that nation as depicted in Exodus under the leadership of Moses. The Amarna Age (1400–1360 B.C.) was a highly literary age. Why Moses could not have recorded the experiences that are found in the books of Exodus, Leviticus, Numbers and Deuteronomy (with the exception of chapter 34) is difficult to comprehend when miners were already writing inscriptions at Serabit Kadim around 1750 B.C. A number of different types of script were available in the days of Moses. Moses could have written the book of Genesis utilizing written records handed down by previous generations and as far as his own life was concerned he could write from personal experience.

While it is true that the Old Testament does not contain historical writing in the tradition as it has obtained during the past two centuries, that does not justify the stance of modern historical criticism that the statements in the Pentateuch and other historical books are not factual. Nor does it justify the assertions made about Adam, Noah, Abraham, Isaac, Jacob, Joseph, Moses, Aaron, Joshua, the various judges, Eli, Samuel, Saul, David, Solomon, Elijah, Elisha and many other personalities as being incorrectly reported. The methodology employed by critical scholars makes the Old Testament an unreliable book and renders it impossible for ordinary lay readers to understand the books

[9]Used by permission. Moody Press, Moody Bible Institute of Chicago.

Genesis to I Samuel as documents that purport to set forth straightforward narrative.

Archaeology in the last 150 years has rendered a valuable service to the biblical student in that it has proven time after time the accuracy of historical statements. One radical theory after another has been repudiated by the findings of the spade. For illustration, let the reader consult the article by Kline, "Is the History of the Old Testament Accurate?" Various peoples alluded to in Genesis and once regarded by negative critics as legendary have been discovered by archaeology to be the flesh and blood people the Scriptures state they were. The Hittites are a famous example as are the Horites, now shown to be the Hurrians who played an important part in the history of Mesopotamia.

The interpretation of Old Testament history proposed by modern critical scholarship, following the presupposition of literary, form and redaction criticism, basically antisupernaturalistic, contradicts the understanding the New Testament has given of historical personalities, events and interpretations. If the New Testament writers, including Jesus, were mistaken in their grasp of Old Testament history, what shall we say about their doctrinal assertions? A study of Acts 7, the speech of Stephen, a man described as filled with the Holy Spirit, clearly indicates that Stephen held to an understanding of Old Testament history accepted in religious circles prior to the adoption of various types of sophisticated criticism. The latter informs the general reader that the text does not mean what it says nor does it say what it means. The author of the eleventh chapter of Hebrews also evinces an understanding of Old Testament history that is out of harmony with the conclusions of higher critics regarding its interpretation. In statements by Christ and in Paul's writings, references are made to

Genesis and Exodus which rule out the critical reconstructions of Genesis 1-11; Genesis 12-50 and Exodus 1-40. Dr. Ira Price, former professor of Semitics at the University of Chicago, in his contribution to Monser's *Cross Reference Bible* has listed seventy-seven incidents in Genesis, thirty-three in Exodus and eight in Numbers that clearly show that the New Testament writers accepted events and statements attributed to Yahweh and to Moses as described. Under no circumstances can the critical interpretation of history, often nothing more than allegorization, be harmonized with the New Testament. The acceptance of higher critical interpretation of Old Testament history seriously jeopardizes the reliability and integrity of Christ and the apostles whom He promised "to guide in all truth." The result of the critical interpretation as stated by the noted Old Testament scholar Hans Wolff is that the Old Testament in Europe is no longer read in the pulpit nor are its assertions taken seriously!

7
Literary Criticism and Biblical Poetry

The Old Testament contains two basic types of literature: prose and poetry. Each has its own specific characteristics and subdivisions. According to many critical scholars, poetry postdates in its origin and written form the prose narratives of the Old Testament. However, this is a stance which is not supported by the evidence of Near Eastern literature.

Most of the poetic material in the Old Testament is found in the Psalms, Proverbs, Song of Solomon, Job (Chapters 3–42:6), parts of Ecclesiastes and large sections of the sixteen prophetical books. Examples of poetry are found in Genesis; the poem of Lamech sung to his two wives may be one of the earliest on record. Genesis 49, containing the curses and blessings spoken by dying Jacob, is largely in poetic form. The song of Miriam in Exodus 15 is another example of poetry embedded in books mainly narrative and historical in character. Moses was a poet as may be seen from Psalm 90 and chapters 30–33 of Deuteronomy.

The Psalms contain examples of Hebrew poetry dating from Moses (Psalm 90) till the exilic period (Psalm 137). The five books into which the psalms are divided are collected over a long period of time. The superscriptions of the psalms ascribe seventy-three to David, two to Solomon, eleven to the Sons of Korah, twelve to Asaph, one to Ethan. No author is mentioned in the case of fifty psalms. The superscriptions, whenever found, always constitute the first verse in the Hebrew text of a psalm. Eighteen of the Davidic psalms also state the occasion for the writing of the poem. If the authenticity of these superscriptions is accepted, the time of their origin would be established and in the case of the Davidic psalms they would be related to David's life. On the basis of the superscriptions more than fifty percent of the psalter would come from the eleventh and tenth centuries respectively, Israel's golden age.

One of the developments of the critical approach to the Old Testament was the rejection of the authenticity and the reliability of the psalm superscriptions. Critical scholars explain them as the first erroneous attempts at literary criticism by Jewish students in the days prior to the translation of the Septuagint. In the early decades of the twentieth century most of the psalms were placed by critical scholars in the postexilic period, with many psalms assigned to the second century B.C. ranking with Daniel among the latest literary products of Judaism.

However, as a result of archaeological discoveries there has been a considerable reversal of scholarly opinion about the date or origin of the psalms. The alphabetic clay tablets found at Ugarit, or Rash Shamra, reveal the fact that poetry was early in use at this ancient city which was destroyed by the Sea People about 1200 B.C. In the Ugaritic alphabetic cuneiform tablets three major Caananite epics were found: the Baal, Aqhat and Keret epics. They reveal their affinity with Hebrew poetry. In these epics one can find meters, varieties of parallelism, pairs of parallel synonyms, phrases, and what were evidently stock similes, which also occur in biblical poetry. This evidence has now led to a complete reversal for dating the Psalms, so that a scholar like Weiser is willing to recognize premonarchial psalms.

Present day critical scholars do not believe that the psalms are "God-breathed" or "God-spirated" but that in the Psalms we simply have either the responses of individual men to various emotional experiences or the reflections of men dealing with problems. However, the New Testament view requires the belief that each psalm was inspired by God and that in the Psalms we hear the voice of God. Throughout the psalter man listens to what God has to tell him and not merely what man is saying to God. If the latter were the case, readers of the Psalms could never be certain about the reliability and certainty of many declarations, teachings and assurances contained in them. Or if the Psalms merely contain the reflections of pious men, it would mean that at best we possess human speculations, hopes and dreams.

Modern scholars who deny the authenticity of psalm superscriptions have rejected statements about the authorship of these poems. In the New Testament, Peter in Acts 2:30 spoke of David as a true prophet. It is the testimony of the New Testament that David was a medium for God's inspired Word. Thus the plan of the temple was made known to David in writing from the Lord (I Chron. 28:19). This is the first biblical context indicating that David was the recipient of divine revelation. David became "the sweet singer of Israel" (II Sam. 23:1). In II Sam. 23:2 David stated that he had the words of God on his tongue so that the Holy Spirit spoke by him. It is not certain that David was always aware that he was writing under the Spirit's guidance. According to the titles, David wrote seventy-three psalms

101

with two anonymous ones being assigned to him by the New Testament.

The psalm titles are old, predating the Septuagint around 200 B.C.; in fact, some of the terms in the superscriptions were no longer understood by the Septuagint translators. Poetic compositions embedded in pre-exilic poetry show a similar use of author titles (Hab. 3:1; Isa. 38:9; II Sam. 1:17,23). Psalms sixteen, thirty-two and one hundred ten, which in the Hebrew text have David as author, are ascribed by Christ and Paul to David. By scriptural analogy Psalms two, ninety-five, ninety-six, one hundred five and one hundred six are also ascribed to David.

David's name is famous in the Old Testament period because music and song are closely associated with him. Chronicles is explicit in stating that David gathered temple choirs and composed psalms for them (I Chron. 16:4,5; 25:1–5). That David had the poetic gift is shown by his masterful elegy, "The Poem of the Bow" composed on the occasion of Saul's and Jonathan's deaths. The internal evidence in the Davidic psalms can in most instances be fitted into some phase of David's life as set forth in I Chronicles.

Recent Trends in Psalm Interpretation
Professor Guthrie in his study, *The Song of Israel* (1966) has shown how recent developments in the study of the Psalms have challenged two basic assumptions formerly held: 1. The Davidic authorship has been generally surrendered and cannot be harmonized with most critical studies proposed in the last four decades; 2. The contention that psalms were written late but that they nevertheless were the products of individual literary activity. When the authentic nucleus and the authority of a psalm had been determined

102

the older critical scholars proceeded to explain a psalm in terms of its ideas, theological concepts and the religious experience that was responsible for the writing of the psalm. As a result of recent work, Guthrie claims, these positions are no longer held.

In recent decades a more radical form of criticism has been developed. More sophisticated methods are supposed to be in vogue, which forbid reading into a poem our attitudes and viewpoints. Israel's poetry can no longer be considered the efforts of individual poets, but must be regarded as the expression of the worshiping community.

The new approaches to the psalms interpretation have been influenced by advances in archaeology, philology and the history of religions and related disciplines. According to Guthrie the psalms come from a culture which was pre-scientific, where mythology instead of philosophy determined what people believed. The world of the psalm writers was much different than our times, so it is claimed that the psalms must be understood in the light of the culture current at the time of their origination.

One of the influences undergirding the new understanding of the Psalter is the alleged borrowing from Near Eastern psalmody. Zimmern, Langdon, Stummer and Cummings made available the rich psalm literature of the Tigris-Euphrates Valley, including Sumerian, Babylonian, and Assyrian psalms. In Assyria the psalm literature was intimately connected with the cultus at the great temples. Gadd, an Assyriologist, contended for the great influence of Babylonia on the hymnic literature of the Old Testament. The Egyptologists Erman, Breasted, and Sethe made the same claim for the psalms found in Egyptian literature. In Egypt the psalms likewise were related to the cultus at the temples. In 1922 the Society for Old Testament Studies

103

sponsored a special volume, *The Psalmists*, in which a number of contributions by British and German scholars not only emphasized that parallels could be found in Near Eastern literature for the various genres but also stressed the structural composition of particular types of psalms. G. R. Driver and G. Widengreen pointed out the similarity of the thanksgiving hymns to examples in Egyptian literature. It is an unproven theory that the Old Testament psalms were influenced by those from Assyria and Egypt.

With the discovery of the Rash Shamrah texts of 1929 and following many scholars became convinced that Israelite religion was indebted to the poetic materials found at Ugarit. More significant parallels were believed to be found in the Ugaritic epics than in Accadian or Egyptian literature. Albright, Montgomery, Harris, Patten, Dahood, Gordon and other scholars assert that a comparison with portions of Ugaritic poetry reveal that the Hebrew poets appropriated phrases, sets of synonyms and poetical ideas. Thus it is claimed that Psalm 29 was literally taken from Ugaritic, the only difference being that the Hebrew poem has the name of Yahweh while the Ugaritic original uses Baal. However, it should be stated that while many words and expressions in Psalm 29 are found in Ugaritic poetry, nowhere among the available Ugaritic texts is there a poem similar to Psalm 29!

A comparison of Hebrew psalms with those of the Near East will reveal in both groups the language of individual and social worship, the devotional mood, the desire and petitions for establishing fellowship and a right relationship with deity, yet the discerning reader will notice a great difference between Hebrew poetry and that of its neighbors. Leslie believes that a comparative study of the religious poetry of the Near East will convince the unbiased reader of the superiority of Hebrew psalms. The latter manifests an incomparably higher level of religious and spiritual insight.

A second trend in psalm studies in the twentieth century was the place assigned to the cultus in the production of the psalms. Because in Sumeria, Babylonia, Assyria, Egypt and Ugarit the psalms are intimately connected with the religious temple, it was assumed that Israelite psalmic literature was to be explained totally in terms of the cultus. On the strength of the existence of a Near Eastern psalmic literature, some Old Testament scholars are willing to admit that there were psalms in Israel of a pre-exilic provenance (i.e. before 587 B.C.). The Scandinavian scholar Mowinckel argued that practically all psalms had their origin in connection with the cultus and were thus intended for rendition in the regular and officially approved services of the Temple. This assumption would eliminate certain psalms composed by individuals whom God inspired to write in connection with some special occasion in the life of the poet or composer.

A third trend in psalm studies combining the two features just discussed is the use of form criticism. Gunkel as has already been stated was the father of form criticism which he first developed in connection with the Book of Genesis. His first studies in the area of psalmic poetry was *Ausgewahlte Psalmen,* (Selected Psalm), published in 1904. It was, however, in the last part of his life that Gunkel concentrated on Old Testament poetry publishing his commentary on *Die Psalmen* (1926) and *Die Einleitung in die Psalmen* in 1933. During a period of twenty-five years he centered his attention on psalm types (*Gattungen*) and endeavored to establish their distinctive characteristics as well as their historical development. He took his cue from Herder, who had claimed that religious poetry was always

105

suited to the situation, for which each kind of poetry had a certain type of convention of literary form which usage had fixed.

Gunkel's Contribution to Psalm Interpretation

Gunkel was also convinced that the religious poetry in Israel had behind it a long historical development. He argued that religious poetry began with an oral stage in Israelite history and reached the peak of its development at the time of the exile. Most of the psalms in their present form he believed had been composed during the postexilic period. According to Gunkel many psalms revealed a mixture of types which he believed had been composed from older forms. One of the results of Old Testament interpretation was that Gunkel dated many psalms much earlier than had those critics who had had a penchant for the Maccabean (165 B.C.) dating of many psalms without, however, raising doubts about the late dating (after 400 B.C.) assigned the compilation of the Psalter.

Gunkel considered each psalm a fragment of ancient Israelite life. He sought to penetrate a psalm to its setting in the actual worship life (*Sitz-im-Leben*) in Israel. These various worship settings gradually created types (*Gattungen*). Since there are many and various kinds of worship occasions Israel must have had different types of psalms. This resulted in each piece of sacred poetry being written for a certain kind or type of occasion, and distinct with its own unique indications. Moreover, each genre is alleged to have had its own history, including both secular and religious expression. According to Gunkel the various types remained distinct until about 500 B.C., when they began to meet and mingle in particular psalms.

Gunkel felt that the primary question to ask about a particular psalm is: what is it intended to do, instead of, what is its date, and who wrote it? Thus he had three objectives in mind in psalm interpretation: 1. To place the literature into type classifications; 2. To determine the history of each type; and 3. To establish the life situation (*Sitz-im-Leben*) that gave rise to the literature. The *Sitz-im-Leben* that gave rise to each psalm was Israel's cultus.

At first six major and six minor classes were identified by Gunkel. His final classification, however, recognized five major and five minor types: 1. Hymns of praise; 2. National laments; 3. Royal psalms; 4. Individual laments; 5. Thanksgiving of the individual. To these were added five minor types: 6. Songs of Pilgrimage; 7. Thanksgiving of the nation; 8. Wisdom poems; 9. Torah liturgies; and 10. Mixed psalms.

The thinking and classification by Gunkel inspired a host of Old Testament scholars to work with and apply his views to the poetry of the Old Testament. Scholars like Mowinckel, Kittel, Schmidt, Leslie, Weiser, Kraus, Westermann and others, each developed his own particular classification of the psalms. A fair analysis of the Psalter would reveal that there is a certain indefiniteness about the psalms which defies classification. Undoubtedly this lack of definiteness is caused by the timeless and universal characteristics of these God-inspired poems.

Lack of Critical Agreement on Fundamental Issues

Great diversity of opinion exists on the part of Old Testament scholars regarding the validity and reliability of form criticism as a hermeneutical methodology in Psalm interpretation because of contradictory views regarding literary genre and *Sitz-im-Leben*. According to Mowinckel the majority of psalms were written for a New Year festival that is supposed to have been celebrated in ancient Israel which came about the time of the equinox when rain ended the summer drought. At this festival the enthronement of Yahweh as king of the universe was commemorated in the Jerusalem Temple. This practice, it is conjectured, was borrowed from the Babylonians who are known to have celebrated such a festival.

Arthur Weiser similarly reacted to Gunkel's work by claiming that the latter had not determined the right life situation for the psalms. While Weiser associates this poetry with the cultus, he argued against outside influence and proposed that Israelite poetry was dependent on a festival of covenant renewal which was absolutely unique. Weiser consequently has psalms composed in the pre-monarchial period around 1200 B.C. Most of the psalms he claims had their origin in a covenant renewal festival. This covenant was the one Yahweh made with Israel at Mt. Sinai. When Joshua was about to die, he called the Israelites to Shechem, where he urged the people to renew the covenant mediated through Moses. That such a renewal took place every year is not recorded in the Old Testament and therefore Weiser is not dealing with facts but with theory when he claims that such a renewal festival was held annually.

Hans-Joachim Kraus has proposed still another *Sitz-im-Leben* for the Psalms. In his large two volume work on *The Psalms*, following the positions of a number of German scholars, Alt, Noth, and von Rad, Kraus contended that at least three formative elements played a part in the cultic traditions that were responsible for the Psalms. He also assumes that the songs of the Old Testament come from a cultic setting. While recognizing the significance of the "tent festival" and the covenant renewal festival, he also stressed the importance of the establishment of the Davidic kingdom and the covenant Yahweh made with David.

Contemporary studies of the Psalms are to a large extent the result of Gunkel's work. Many of these current publications object to his views and propose new theories. A same psalm is interpreted differently by the various psalm specialists, leaving the general reader therefore confused as to how reliable their interpretations are since they disagree on what is basic in the newer studies; namely, the life situation that produced a psalm.

Modern critical scholarship has generally rejected the New Testament teaching that in the Psalms there are predictions about Israel's Messiah. Jesus showed Cleophas and his friend that the Messiah had to suffer but then would be glorified on the basis of the law, the prophets and the psalms (Luke 24:44). Opinions differ as to the number of psalms that should be so classified. The major ones which seem to speak directly of the Messiah are: two, sixteen, twenty-two, forty, forty-five, sixty-nine, seventy-two, eighty-nine and one hundred ten. If we include all to which the New Testament refers in the life of Christ, one would also add: eight, forty-one, sixty-eight, one hundred two, one hundred nine and one hundred eighteen.

Among all the books of antiquity, none has had a more powerful appeal to the human heart than the Psalms. No other biblical book reflects such varities of religious experience. The experiences of the individual are linked to the corporate life of Israel. Because of the varieties of religious experience found in them, the Psalms possess a timeless quality which has made this book the favorite of both Jew and Christian and has been a favorite in every age of history. Earnest study of the inspired songs of Israel will lead to a deeper understanding of God's ways and His glory. Their use will further lead the individual to a more active communion with God.

8
Higher Criticism and the Wisdom Literature

In Old Testament times three classes of religious people were active in Israel: prophets, priests and wise men. This is clear from Jer. 18:18 where the prophet asserted: "When they said, Come let us make plots against Jeremiah, for the law shall not perish from the priests, nor counsel from the wise, nor the word from the prophet."

The prophets were not conciliatory in their approach to the people and often antagonized them because of their condemnatory strictures, necessary and well deserved. Ranstoun contends that:

It is customary, and with justification, to regard the prophets as the most illustrious exponents of the Hebrew religious spirit. But it may be doubted if the influence of these spiritual experts would have been permanent and far reaching apart from the work of the wise men in popularizing their ideals and creating among the ordinary people a spirit sympathetic with them.[1]

The wise men may be said to have supplemented the work of the prophets and preserved their teachings. The wise men constituted an important class in the advancement of the Hebrew religion. The books of Job, Proverbs,

Ecclesiastes and a number of Psalms, such as Psalms one, ten, fourteen, nineteen, thirty-seven, ninety, one hundred four, one hundred seven, one hundred forty-eight and others, as well as short passages in other books, are classified as wisdom literature and may be said to be the literary productions of wise men. Among the Apocrypha, Ecclesiasticus and the Wisdom of Solomon belong to this type of literary genre.

The kings and leaders of Israel needed wisdom, since they were required to make important decisions in political and social realms. Thus Joshua, David and Solomon are depicted as receiving wisdom from God in rendering official decisions. The Messianic King of the future is described as one who deals wisely and who will judge impartially because He is endowed with wisdom. A special class of men known as wise men came into existence during the days of the monarchy. By Jeremiah's time they seem to have taken a place next to the priests and prophets in Judah. Law and prophecy came directly from Yahweh and in the highest sense are His Word. Wisdom proceeds from man and is the product of his observations and experiences. Israelite wisdom, however, does recognize that the fear of God is the foundation and beginning of true wisdom (Ps. 111:10; Prov. 9:10; Ecc. 12:13). Although the sayings of wise men represent human reflection, those recorded in Scripture have received the stamp of God's approval by inspiration of the Holy Spirit. A beautiful encomium on wisdom is found in Job 28:12-27. In Prov. 1:20-33 and in chapters 7,8,9:1-12, wisdom is personified, an idea taken over in the apocryphal wisdom literature.

The utterances of the wise men are represented by parable (II Sam. 14:4-11), precept (Prov. 24:27-29), proverb (Prov. 24:23-26), riddle (Prov. 1:6), the story of real life and its lesson (Prov. 24:30-34). Other forms of wisdom literature

112

would be Jotham's fable (Judges 9:7–20), Samson's riddle or dark saying (Judges 14:14), Nathan's parable and those enacted by the wise men of Tekoa and a certain prophet (II Sam. 12:1–7; I Kings 20:35–43) and the fable told by King Jehoash (II Kings 14:9–10).

The author of I Kings portrays Solomon as an extremely wise man. It is stated that his wisdom was greater than that of the wise men of the East and Egypt. He was expert in botany and zoology; the Bible credits him with 3,000 proverbs and 1,005 songs; he is mentioned as the author of the Song of Songs, his greatest song (Song of Sol. 1:1), with most of the Book of Proverbs (Prov. 1:1), Ecclesiastes (1:1,12) and two Psalms (72,127). People came from various countries of the Fertile Crescent to hear the wisdom of Solomon (I Kings 10:25).

Erroneous Views about Old Testament Wisdom
Literature

Critical scholarship had adopted erroneous views about the wisdom literature of the Old Testament and the place of it in Israel's religion. Refusing to abide by sound principles of interpretation and motivated by skepticism, critical scholars have refused to accept clear statements of the Bible regarding Solomon's wisdom and the fact that he gave literary expression of this wisdom in a number of writings. Hence critical scholars conclude that just as Moses became synonymous with the Law and all later laws were ascribed to Moses, so Solomon became the "patron saint" of all succeeding wise men or sages. Instead of engaging a well-known scholar to write an introduction for a collection of proverbs and philosophical statements, authors of wisdom writings are said to have assumed anonymity and credited Solomon with them.

A further claim is made by those who hold a faulty view of

113

biblical revelation and inspiration to the effect that when Solomon chose wisdom and decided to pursue it, this action resulted in forcing the prophets into seclusion. Thus Robison wrote: "The wisdom of observation obliged the wisdom of inspiration to give ground. From henceforth there was in the Hebrew nation a firmly established school whose teachings, as we would say, were based on empiricism or 'common sense.'"[2]

Critical scholarship also maintains that the prophets were impatient with the wise men, even though it was a wise man who wrote: "Where there is no vision, the people cast off restraint" (Prov. 29:18). Some critical scholars have depicted Hebrew wisdom as rationalistic in spirit and inimical to a true religion of revelation. The prophets, described as having mystical experiences, believed that truth came as divine revelation. However, a proper understanding of biblical prophecy requires the recognition of the fact that the prophets were not the originators of their preaching and writing. Their message was from God and therefore was "the Word of God." The wise men are never described as opponents of prophets and are falsely pitted against the prophets.

The wise men in Israel are said to have concerned themselves with the practical realities of life. Righteousness was conceived of as a virtue that brought its own reward although the wise men did not scorn good for its own sake. Unlike the prophets, the wise men were not classified as men of action but rather as thinkers or philosophers. They pondered the problems of life in a dispassionate manner. The wisdom writings of the Old Testament contain the crystallization of their thinking.

Wisdom set forth in proverbs, parables, allegories and other extended forms did not first originate in the postexilic

114

period. Incorrectly, critical scholarship has assigned the wisdom literary genre to the latest strata of Old Testament writings, a position it is claimed is shown also by the presence of Ecclesiastes, Proverbs and Job among the books of the third division of the Hebrew Old Testament canon. In attempting to visualize the manner in which the wise men arose in Israel, critical scholars believe that in the wisdom literature emanating from the Near East there are insights that might help to answer that question. Egypt, Sumeria and Babylonia have furnished examples of various types of wisdom literature, some dating back to the third millennium B.C. Among this literature there were two main types: 1. prudential wisdom, usually expressed in brief sentences, and 2. reflective essays on the significance of life, often of a pessimistic character. The forms of Israelite wisdom literature are alleged to correspond to the literary types of international wisdom.

From Egyptian wisdom literature it appears that young men received training to be important state functionaries of trust and responsibility. At some schools the scribes trained young men in etiquette and gave them moral instruction. At other schools young men could prepare for careers at court. Egyptian students were required to copy sayings of the wise men. Some of these copy sheets have been found. In Babylonia and Assyria wisdom teachers were state functionaries. Some scholars claim the same practice was in vogue in Israel.

The writings of the Old Testament know of wisdom as an international phenomenon, as shown in statements in I Kings 4:31; Obadiah 8; Jer. 49:7, where there are references to the wisdom of Edom and Egypt. To what degree, if any, ancient Near Eastern wisdom literature has affected that of Israel is the big question. Those scholars who have a completely erroneous concept of the nature of the Old Testament canon claim that Hebrew wise men were influenced by other nations in their understanding of Hebrew wisdom. The closest parallel to Egyptian wisdom is found between the Wisdom of Amenemopet and Prov. 22:17-24:22. The latter portion of Proverbs is said to have been based on the thirty chapters of the Wisdom of Amenemopet. A majority of critical scholars have accepted the assertion of certain Egyptologists that Proverbs has relied on Amenemopet for the wisdom thoughts in this passage. The Confraternity version renders Prov. 22:17-21 in the following manner: "The saying of the wise: 'Incline your ear, and hear my words, and apply your heart to my doctrine: for it will be well if you keep them in your bosom, if they all are ready on your lips. That your trust may be in the Lord, I make known to you the words of Amen-em-Ope. Have I not written for you the "Thirty," with counsels and knowledge, to teach you truly how to give a dependable report to one who sends you?'"[3] Here a critical conjecture has been placed into the text itself which is strange procedure for a translation that purports to be a literal rendering of the Hebrew text. The Revised Standard Version and the New English Bible have adopted a vocalization of the Hebrew consonants *shlshm* in Prov. 22:20 which would be the number "thirty" in Hebrew, thus subscribing to the theory of the alleged borrowing of Proverbs from the Egyptian book. However, an analysis of Prov. 22:17-24:22 reveals that there are not actually thirty sayings in that portion.

It is also claimed by critical scholars that the biblical proverbs are dependent on the *Proverbs of Achikar*, a copy of which was made in Aramaic from an Akkadian original and was found in the Jewish Aramaic papyri discovered at

Elephantine in the early part of this century. Parallels to Job and Ecclesiastes are found by some scholars in Egyptian and Mesopotamian literature. No literary survivals of Edomite wisdom literature have as yet been found. Some scholars believe that two sections of Proverbs: 30:1-14, 31:1-9, are of Arabian origin since according to Gen. 25:14 Massa is alluded to as an Arabian tribe.

Except for a few allusions to the covenant, the work of God in history, the doctrine of the election, the Messiah and the Day of Yahweh, many critical scholars claim that a real religious note is absent in Proverbs of the Bible. In the discussion of justice and righteousness in Proverbs, Job and Ecclesiastes, according to these scholars, no difference exists between the presentation of these concepts as expressed in non-Israelite literature. Thus Hooke wrote: "Apart from the replacement of Ea, Shamash, Re and Horus with Yahweh, it might almost appear that Israel's wisdom was one with that of the extra-Israelite world; it should be noted however, that the Apocryphal wisdom literature is explicitly integrated into Jewish faith and practice."[4] Robison asserted about the wisdom literature: "Apart from its place in the Old Testament canon, the Wisdom literature might apply, without qualification, to any people. There is no reflection of national prejudices which are frequent in other books."[5] He also contends that the Wisdom books do not have reference to Jewish history. In Job and Proverbs, Jerusalem is not mentioned at all. References to kings and commandments are so general as supposedly to make it difficult to believe that the people of Israel could express themselves along such lines.

Because of the peculiar type of literature represented by the wisdom genre, critical scholars believe that the writers of wisdom materials in the Old Testament must have traveled extensively which broadened their sympathies. In contact with foreign religions, these wise men realized that the religion of their forefathers had too nationalistic a conception of God. This new insight accordingly led to a new conception of God for His chosen people.

Critical scholarship generally believes that the wisdom literature of the Old Testament belongs to the postexilic period. A number of the wisdom books have been placed into the Greek period (331–63 B.C.). Greek influence has been claimed to have been transmitted to the author of Ecclesiastes. Some critical scholars have gone so far as to claim that hedonistic or stoic teachings were actually incorporated into this book which has been variously interpreted.

A further contention is that the wise men placed little stress on ritualistic religion. Sometimes they were inclined to challenge the working ways of Yahweh among men and they did not hesitate to doubt or question past teachings as expressed in biblical books. The authors of Job and Ecclesiastes came to grips with traditional views and challenged them. The wise men are said to have looked at life with "open and yet reverent eyes."

The Relationship of Hebrew Wisdom Literature to that of the Near East

A great difference exists between Hebrew and pagan wisdom. While pagan wisdom was religious, it had no anchor in the covenant and as Isa. 19:11ff, Ezek. 28:2ff. and Obadiah 8 show, this worldly wisdom is doomed to failure. Some Israelites were guilty of secularism and materialism and their disdain of covenant ideals resulted in a practical atheism which caused Isaiah to exclaim: "Woe unto them that are wise in their own eyes" (29:14).

Hebrew wisdom literature did not contain a philosophical wisdom. Hebrew wise men did not resort to dialectic nor did they express themselves in abstract terminology. Their concern was to teach men to live wisely and to find intellectual satisfaction with Yahweh. Much of the content of Hebrew wisdom literature consisted of maxims of conduct. Solomon had great knowledge of the behavior and characteristics of plants and animals. His proverbs made use of analogies between them and men. Ecclesiastes, Job and the didactic psalms concern themselves with the problems of life and human experience.

While similarities are present between Hebrew wisdom literature and parallels found in Egypt, Ugarit, Babylonia and Sumeria, Hebrew wisdom literature is essentially different. Israel's wisdom literature was determined by its faith in Yahweh, which was responsible for giving it a character all its own. In the Egyptian pantheon, gods of wisdom were worshiped by Egyptians; but by comparison, Yahweh alone is depicted as truly and uniquely wise. His wisdom is shown in creation (Prov. 3:19, Job 38–39). The wisdom of Yahweh provides knowledge as how to live ethically. In Proverbs, wisdom is personified (1:23–33; 8:22–26; 9:1–9). Wisdom personified was with God at creation, through whom creation took place. The early Church Fathers, Luther and a host of exegetes since the days of the Reformation regard the personification of wisdom the same as the *Word* (Logos) of the prologue of St. John's Gospel. This wisdom is said to have been begotten in eternity.

The wisdom of God is seen not only in creation but also in His management of human history (Job 12:13ff.). Apart from Yahweh there can be no true wisdom. "The fear of the Lord is the beginning of wisdom" (Prov. 1:7; 9:10; 15:24; Job 28:28). The highest wisdom that a person can attain is the understanding of the works of Yahweh, especially His judgments (Jer. 9:11; Hos. 14:10). Moses in Deuteronomy states that wisdom is the observation of the law of God. This became a major theme in all subsequent Israelite literature. In comparison with Near Eastern wisdom literature, the Hebrew variety alone is directed explicitly to the problems of the individual. While it is free from peculiarly national traits, it does refer a number of times to God, and the ethical note is strong and prominent.

The Hebrew wisdom literature does not only struggle with the practical problems of life as in Proverbs, but concerns itself with great moral and spiritual issues like the prosperity of the wicked (cf. Ps. 37, 73). Materialism, fatalism and pessimism are rejected in Ecclesiastes and other wisdom passages. The subject of the suffering of the righteous (Job) is discussed. In their clear-sighted practicality the Old Testament wisdom writings are far superior to those pagan texts that the interested reader can find in Pritchard's *Ancient Near Eastern Texts.*

9
True or False Prophecy

The present arrangement of the books of the Hebrew Old Testament is a tripartite one and consists of: 1. The Torah or Law of Moses (five books); 2. The Prophets, divided into two groups: the Former (four books) and Latter Prophets (four books); and 3. The Writings, with a threefold division: three books of poetry (Psalms, Proverbs and Job), the Five Scrolls (Ruth, Ecclesiastes, Lamentations, Song of Solomon, and Esther), and the historical books (Ezra, Nehemiah, Daniel, and I and II Chronicles).

In the Hebrew Bible the books of the Former Prophets include Joshua, Judges, I and II Samuel and I and II Kings. Among the Latter Prophets are found the books of Isaiah, Jeremiah, Ezekiel and the Twelve Minor Prophets as one book. From a literary point of view the books of the Former Prophets actually contain material that normally would be classified as historical. The Septuagint designated these as historical and places them with historical books. The reason why Jewish scholars called them prophetic books was probably due to the fact that prophets were their authors. Among the books of the Latter Prophets, the twelve Minor

121

Prophets is one book and not twelve separate ones as is the case in the Septuagint, Vulgate and in all translations that were influenced either by the Septuagint or the Vulgate. The Book of Daniel, found among the historical books of the third division of the Hebrew canon, was placed with the Major Prophets in the Septuagintal grouping of prophetic books.

In the Latter Prophets we find one of the major types of literary genre exhibited by the Old Testament. In one edition of the Revised Standard Version the sixteen prophetic books occupy 221 pages out of a total of 750 pages, which means that the sixteen prophetic books of the Old Testament comprise thirty percent of the Old Testament. It should, however, be noted that there are references to prophets and prophetic activity in other Old Testament books.

From the days of Joshua till the time of Eli "there was no open vision in Israel" (I Sam. 3:1) because during the time of the judges, the priesthood through whom Yahweh instructed His people, had become corrupt. The Israelites were no longer influenced by the examples that the ritual and ceremonies were intended to convey. In this crisis God introduced a new moral power that would affect the people and improve conditions. God called Samuel, a Levite and member of the Kohathite family (I Chron. 6:28) and most likely a priest, to reform the degenerated priesthood. With Samuel the prophetic office assumed an importance not heretofore evident in Israel. The inception both for the prophetic and regal orders is already found in Deut. 13:1, 18:20 and 18:18. Mention is made in I Samuel of prophetic companies or guilds that were founded under the leadership of Samuel. These companies or colleges of prophets were found in the following cities: Ramah (I Sam. 19:19,20), Bethel (II Kings 2:3), Jericho (2:5), Gilgal (4:38), and in other places (6:1). Dr. Unger believes that these colleges, comparable to theological schools, furnished men for the prophetic office until the end of the close of the Old Testament canon. He is of the opinion that "their chief subject of study was, no doubt, the law and its interpretation; oral as distinctive from symbolical, teaching being henceforth tacitly transferred from the priestly to the prophetical order. Subsidiary subjects of instruction were music and sacred poetry, both of which had been connected with prophecy from the time of Moses (Ex. 15:20) and the judges (Judg. 4:4; 5:11)."[1]

The prophets were primarily men who were "forthtellers," that is, they set forth God's will and demands to their fellow men. Even when the prophet used charades and mimicking, as did Jeremiah and Ezekiel, his objective was to bring a message of warning or encouragement from God to his contemporaries. Thus every prophet was primarily a proclaimer of God's will as stated in Amos 1-2. The demands and requirements of the Mosaic law were the frame of reference for the prophets in their evaluation of the actions of the people. The prophets were not chiefly concerned with giving a defense of small details of the law, but were involved in castigating the sins of the people. Idolatry was the most serious and prevalent sin in Israel and Judah. Worshiping gods of the neighboring peoples was a violation of the very first commandment of the Decalogue. It was pointless to emphasize any other laws of God if the first commandment was not heeded. Ritualism and worship

[1]Used by permission. Moody Press, Moody Bible Institute of Chicago.

in the temple were worthless if God was not served and his ethical principles followed. Mere formalism is rebuked many times in the prophetic writings.

Moses as a prophet and representative of God had set forth ethical and moral demands. When the children of Israel departed from the Mosaic standard, as so often happened, the prophets warned the people against disobeying God's commandments and announced the consequent punishments that God had threatened in Deuteronomy (chapters 28–30). The minatory messages were delivered to produce repentance on the part of the people of Israel. In the prophetic books there are also messages of encouragement for those faithful to God.

One of the identifying signs of prophetic revelation vouchsafed to the prophets was its progressive revelatory nature. From the time of Moses to Malachi, God was revealing Himslf more fully through the truths enunciated in the writings of the prophets. Prophetic preaching was always in harmony with the Law of Moses (Deut. 13:5), but God also used the prophets for making known ethical insights and for adding new doctrinal material to provide a fuller understanding of God's teachings.

Not only were the prophets "forthtellers" but they were also foretellers, predicting future events. Prediction was often a characteristic of prophetic messages, and according to Deut. 18:9ff. it was to belong to the very essence of the prophetic office. Israel was warned by Moses about consulting pagan soothsayers in Canaan, whom today we would label as fortunetellers. Instead Israel was to heed those men whom the Lord appointed, such as Moses, and these men were to be judged by the accuracy of their predictions (Deut. 18:22) which was an imporant element of prophecy. Outstanding among the predictive statements of the prophets were those relative to the Messiah and His kingdom. The New Testament affirms in many passages that the coming of the Messiah was foretold by the prophets of old. Matthew has the formula nearly fifty times, "this happened that it might be fulfilled that which was spoken by the prophet . . ." Predictions about the great redemptive events in the life of the Messiah were identified by New Testament believers and writers as fulfilled in Jesus of Nazareth.

The Old Testament literature distinguishes between true and false prophets. In I Kings 22, Micaiah, the son of Imlah, and Zedekiah, the son of Chenaanah are described as opposing each other. In Jeremiah 33, Hananiah, a false prophet, confronted the prophet Jeremiah. How could the true prophet be distinguished from the false? Some scholars have suggested that ecstasy was a sign of a false prophet. However in Samuel we have a number of examples of ecstasy mentioned as characterizing Saul and others and no word of condemnation is uttered because of these ecstatic manifestations. Isaiah and Ezekiel seem to have had ecstatic experiences. Other scholars have claimed that professionalism was a mark of a false prophet. Yet the Old Testament does not support this view, for Samuel and Nathan certainly were professional prophets, being associated with the court. Both Deuteronomy 13 and 18 give a negative test for determining a false prophet. If a prophet makes an unconditional prediction and it is not fulfilled, it would be obvious that he was not a spokesman for God. However, sometimes it did happen that a false prophet's prediction materialized. In Deuteronomy 13 we find a further test given to distinguish between a true and false prophet, namely, a theological one. The false prophets would encourage people to go "after other gods which thou hast not known" (13:2), thus uttering "rebellion against the

125

Lord your God, who brought you out of the land of Egypt" (Verses 5, 10 RSV). Any prophet who did not speak in harmony with Mosaic teaching was, therefore, a false prophet.

With the division of the kingdom (931 B.C.) there seems to have been an efflorescence of prophecy. Between 930–722 B.C., twenty-three different prophets are referred to, in most cases only their names are given. In I Kings 13; 20:1–13 and II Chronicles there are also references to unnamed prophets. Between 722 B.C. and 400 B.C., in Judah, fourteen prophets and one prophetess (Hulda) are mentioned.

The chronological order of the writing prophets might be given as follows:

1. Joel, Obadiah (ninth century B.C.)

2. Jonah, Hosea, Amos, Isaiah and Micah (eighth century B.C.)

3. Jeremiah, Nahum, Zephaniah, Habakkuk (seventh century B.C.)

4. Ezekiel and Daniel (sixth century B.C.)

5. Haggai, Zechariah, Malachi (sixth and fifth centuries B.C.)

Critical Approach to the Prophetic Writings and Prophecy
Two major viewpoints are currently represented regarding the understanding of prophecy in Old Testament literature—naturalistic and supernaturalistic. The former regards prophets and prophecy almost exclusively from a human viewpoint and thus frequently rejects or obscures the divine element of revelation and inspiration. By contrast, the biblical vantage point regards both the human and the divine factors that are involved in the activity of the prophet and his message.

Those scholars who espouse the naturalistic approach to

126

prophecy merely regard it as a normal development and the prophetic phenomena are interpreted as merely political and social manifestations. Prophets surveyed contemporary developments of their time and proclaimed messages based on insight and analysis of current events. The prophetic books of the Hebrew Old Testament bear the names of specific individuals but these ascriptions are not accepted by higher critics as belonging to these writings. In most cases the prophetic writings are considered works of anonymous writers. The second part of the canon, it is claimed, was only formed around the year 200 A.D.

Direct revelation by God, which is implied in the phrase: "Thus says the Lord" or "Saying of Yahweh" is not accepted in the sense intended, nor are those portions of the prophetic writings that deal with the future and make predictions. Since it is claimed by higher critics that prediction by human beings is impossible, predictive assertions must have been written after their fulfillment. Modern negative biblical criticism does not regard the Bible as containing reliable primary source documents for the historical facts recorded concerning prophets and their messages.

Neither does modern negative biblical criticism accept many statements in the historical books relative to the life of Moses. According to Pentateuchal writings, Moses was a Hebrew who lived in the fifteenth pre-Christian century or at the latest in the thirteenth century B.C. He is not merely a "prophet" by retrojection, but Moses said and did the things that are ascribed to him in Exodus, Leviticus, Numbers, and Deuteronomy.

While many critical scholars believe in revelation, their definition of this concept is inadequate because they limit revelation to acts of God to which there were human responses. Although these biblical scholars teach that God

127

acted by a number of mighty acts, tney simultaneously hold that the human response to these acts can be wrong because these interpretations are based on a human analysis of what happened. The concept of God communicating thoughts and ideas to His chosen servants is considered untenable. Nor is the contention acceptable that the content of prophetic preaching, which was sometimes set forth in words, came directly from God. God gave Moses interpretations that the Pentateuch depicts as constituting messages from Yahweh Himself.

To understand the nature of much Old Testament prophecy, it is necessary to examine instructions that God gave Moses in Deuteronomy. The problem of the antiquity and authorship of the Pentateuch, a literary issue for the last two hundred years, is basic to a consideration of the prophets and their writings. The Four Source Documentary Hypothesis claims that the Pentateuch is a composite of four separate documents: "J," "E," "D," and "P."

The Pentateuch as a literary composition, according to critical scholarship, was only completed by 400 B.C. While the proponents of this theory concede that Moses was an historical figure, they contend that the literature relating to his person is partly historical and partly fictional, since much in the Pentateuch reflects the "memory of Israel" and therefore cannot be reliable. According to the Documentary Hypothesis much of the material in the Law of Moses is contemporary with a number of prophets, in some cases data in the Pentateuch would come after their time. The dating of the Pentateuch is crucial for the interpretation of the prophetical writings.

Archaeological discoveries pertaining to the suzerainty covenants found in the Hittite historical documents (1600–1200 B.C.) as examined by Mendenhall, show that Deuteronomy compares more favorably with fifteenth century documents than with seventh century writings. Various books of the Old Testament ascribe the Pentateuch to Moses as does also the New Testament. Thus Moses is said to have deposited the law by the ark (Deut. 31:9) and commanded its public reading (Deut. 31:11). If the law was placed in the ark, it was preserved as a part of the Pentateuch, and then would serve as the basis for future evaluations by the prophets, a position the J. E. D. P. theory does not allow. Because of a disbelief in direct revelation and the possibility that a prophet could foretell future events, critics have divided many books, such as Isaiah into chapters 1-39, 40-55 and 56-66; in fact, some scholars claim many different individuals contributed to "the anthology of Isaiah." Portions of the books of Jeremiah, Ezekiel, Amos and Micah, are denied to these prophets and instead are ascribed to later writers. The tendency has been to deny the integrity of the men originally considered by Jews and Christians to be the authors of many prophetic books. Also because of the denial of the miraculous, Jonah and Daniel have been rejected as historical personages who in the books bearing their names recorded their experiences. These prophetical writings have been assigned to a much later time than the events that are described in Jonah (fifth century) and Daniel (second century B.C.).

Form criticism, which has been applied to the historical and poetic literature of the Old Testament has also been applied to prophetic literature. This may be said to be one of the main current critical ways of dealing with the prophetic books. With the justification of this approach validated in the eyes of many scholars, the practice of Bernard Duhm and others, of breaking the prophetic oracles into separate oracles and poetical compositions, became warranted. Form critics dealing with the prophetic literature contended that the written prophetic books of the Old Testament were not actually the products of one writer, as once held, but rather compilations of small units, some oracles originating with the prophet while others were additions by the prophet's disciples. According to this reasoning, ultimately many prophetic books are the works of "a school of writers."

The classic exposition of this view may be found in Theodore Robinson's *Prophecy and the Prophets in Ancient Israel* (1923). Gunkel contended that the prophets added to their short oracles, materials arrived at as a result of their meditation. The prophets under ecstatic experience are said to have given utterance to brief passages. Just as Gunkel assumes the groupings of early legends into story cycles prior to their being written, so Robinson believed that the process of collecting prophetic oracles was partially achieved by a prophet's disciples, who arranged them into a cycle of prophetic tradition.

Modern critical scholarship has followed the lead of Gunkel and Robinson and has depicted the prophets of Israel primarily as preachers or speakers of God's message. The prophetic sermons were delivered by word of mouth and the oral character of their messages was stamped on their surviving words. The form critical approach to the prophetical literature has become one of the leading emphases in current Old Testament studies. This means that Isaiah, Jeremiah, Ezekiel, and the twelve Minor Prophets were actually not the authors of these biblical books, as was formerly assumed. McCarthy in the *New Catholic Encyclopedia* asserts of the "writing prophets":

It was once the practice to call these men, the canonical prophets of the Bible, the "writing" prophets. Although this calls attention

130

to the relative importance of their words as compared to the records of the older *nebi 'im*, where it is the tale of the prophetic activity that is the center of interest, this term is unfortunate because these prophets (except perhaps Ezekiel . . .) were not writers at all. They were essentially preachers who proclaimed God's word to men of their times. The prophetic books as they are in the Bible are actually collections of their sayings preserved by the close associates of the prophets, gathered together and edited over a more or less long period of time, a fact that is important to notice in order to understand the loose organization of the prophetic books.[2]

The position of many Roman Catholic and Protestant scholars is that the prophetic books as they are at present in the Bible are the products of accumulation and growth. In some cases small collections preceded the gathering of disparate sayings with a similar literary form (e.g. the "woes" in Isaiah 5). In the materials collected to make up the prophetic books (Ezekiel, Jeremiah, Isaiah) there appears to be a certain amount of order according to fixed forms and themes: threats against nations, and consolation for Israel. However, it is claimed that even in such instances the scheme is only loosely applied, and in general it is impossible to find a true overall plan in the prophetic books themselves according to which there are any internal links between the literary or historical context.

Bruce Vawter in his *Introduction to the Prophetical Books* points out that in the prophetical books many different literary forms are found. But according to the form critics the proper prophetic form is the oracle. Vawter maintains that in the strictest sense of the word "it is only in the oracles that the prophet spoke precisely as prophet, that is, as one inspired of God."[3] This has unfortunately led

---

[2]From *New Catholic Encyclopedia.* Copyright 1965 McGraw-Hill Book Company. Used with permission of McGraw-Hill Book Company.

scholars to conclude that one must distinguish between what really is a word from God and what is human interpretation in a prophetic book. Thus many statements which formerly were held by biblical students in all branches of Christianity and Judaism prior to the introduction of form criticism, are now rejected as "reflecting" the divine mind.

Those who espouse form criticism declare that the first step for the proper interpretation of the prophetic literature is to determine the limits of literary composition. Harrington, a Roman Catholic scholar who has embraced form criticism as an interpretative methodology, asserts: "It is absolutely essential for an intelligent reading of the prophets that the limits of these units be determined and their literary form identified."[4]

Old Testament prophecy, the critics claim, belongs to the literature of revelation, which means its character must be determined by the conviction that God has communicated His Word (dabhar) to man. The oracular style is said, therefore, to be the outstanding feature of prophetic literature. The most prophetic characteristic is the phrase "Thus says the Lord." Another scheme is "Oracle of Yahweh" (cf. Amos 1:3-2:16). Many of the original oracles were brief (I Kings 21:19), others were longer. Form critics in treating prophetic literature contend that the units of the pre-literary prophets were very short.

While the typical literary genre for the prophetic books was the *oracle*, this in turn is supposed to be divided into a number of sub-genres. Gunkel, as has already been stated, had engaged in some study of prophecy, but he stressed the simplicity of the oracle. Claus Westermann, in his *Grundform Prophetischer Rede* (1960) attacked Gunkel's position as erroneous and endeavored to show the composite nature of the oracles. Westermann distinguished between the oracle of condemnation, which may be uttered against an individual or a group, and the oracle of salvation. The former type has the following structure: commission, accusation, formula of commission, and announcement of punishment (Amos 7:16–17; I Kings 21:17–19). Another variant, according to Westermann, was the oracle of judgment against Israel which had the following pattern: basic accusation, development of accusation, formula of commission, divine intervention and its consequences (Amos 4:1–3: Isa. 8:5–8). In contrast to the oracle of condemnation there was the oracle of salvation, which does not seem to follow a particular literary scheme. Thus the oracle against the nations (Hebrew massah) may use the simple scheme: because of sin, therefore the punishment (Amos 1–2); or it may have the following pattern: symbol or vision, reaction of the prophet, explanation of the vision as punishment, and Yahweh's conclusion.

Many different literary forms are to be found in prophetical literature. Muilenberg in an article dealing with prophetical literature has listed twenty-two different kinds which are found in the sixteen prophetical books.

Form critics have envisioned the formation of the prophetical books in the following manner:

Their words must soon have been written down and we may visualize a primitive prophetical literature circulating in the form of short and separate writings. In the gradual work of collecting and editing, elements were added: earlier collections were sometimes broken up, and the material was finally arranged according to a plan—something very vague—that must be determined (if possible) for each book. The complex genesis of the prophetical books (or many of them) goes far to explain the disconcerting disarray that can confuse and exasperate the reader. The realization, for instance, that the Book of Isaiah is an anthology of sermons or oracles, puts the reader on his guard.[5]

Form critical advocates differ as to the degree to which the actual words and message of the prophecy can be recovered. A scholar like Engnell says that it is not possible at all; another Scandinavian scholar, Bentzen claims that it is extremely difficult, while yet another Scandinavian savant Mowinckel asserts that it is possible.

The form critical school has introduced skepticism into biblical interpretation. It causes the hermeneutical methodology to be characterized by subjectivity, and the beautiful harmony and unity of books like Isaiah, Jeremiah, Ezekiel and the Twelve Minor Prophets are destroyed. The New Testament writers in their quotations from the prophetical writings were completely unaware of the distinctions introduced by the form critics in distinguishing between God's Word and man's within a prophetical book.

10
Can the First Three Gospels Be Trusted?

Nearly all of our information about the life and teachings of Jesus, the instructions which He gave His disciples, and directives concerning His future church, are contained in the four Gospels. The opening verses of the Gospel of Luke indicate the existence during the first century A.D. of a number of accounts on the life of Christ which were known and consulted by St. Luke. Those biographies of Christ that we have in our New Testament were not written as a cooperative effort on the part of the four evangelists but were penned for different groups in various parts of the Roman empire of that day. When Christ was about to leave this earth and ascend into heaven, He gave the command that His followers were to preach the gospel to every creature, teaching and baptizing according to His prior instructions. Christ also had promised His apostles the gift of the Holy Spirit who would bring all teachings to their remembrance and guide them into all truth. The life, crucifixion, resurrection and ascension of Christ became the center of post-Pentecostal church preaching.

The message about the crucified and risen Christ was

initially proclaimed orally. There were probably a number of factors to account for this. Most of the earliest Christians were non-literary individuals, simple people who had enjoyed little formal education. In first century Judaism the oral transmission of tradition was the vogue and the first Christians would naturally share in such transmission. Many Christians also looked for an early return of their Master. For these and other reasons the facts about the life of Jesus were not put into writing. The materials that were incorporated in the four Gospels were composed for teaching and preaching purposes. By repeating the significant features of our Lord's ministry and His accompanying precepts, following the general order of Jesus' biography, the Gospels set forth a body of teaching which may have varied in detail with each recital but which held to the same general content.

That there was a standardized message is shown from a number of New Testament passages. Paul, in mentioning a visit to Jerusalem in 50 A.D. said . . . "I laid before them the gospel, which I preach among the Gentiles" (Gal. 2:2). In another passage Paul wrote to the Corinthians: "the gospel which I preached unto you, which ye also received, wherein also ye stand, by which ye are also saved" (I Cor. 15:1-5). In the Acts of the Apostles there are a number of examples of apostolic preaching from which inferences can be made about the essentials of Christian teaching and preaching. From these samples one may conclude that the facts of Jesus' life constituted the heart of the gospel, which was understood and interpreted to suit the occasion for which it was prepared. The oral gospel which eventually was put into writing in the four Gospels represented a new type of literature. The Gospels are not purely biographies of Jesus, although all that we know about the earthly life of Christ is obtained from them, nor are they sufficiently didactic to be called essays. The writers of the Gospels wanted to use them to effect faith in Christ Jesus. No type of literature similar to the Gospels is found in the Old Testament or in Hellenistic or Roman literature.

Of the many accounts of the life and activities of Jesus penned by various individuals after Pentecost, only four came to be recognized as authoritative or canonical. The early church believed that the first Gospel was written by Matthew Levi, the tax collector: the second Gospel by Mark, an inhabitant of Jerusalem and a companion of Barnabas and Paul; the third Gospel by Luke, a medical doctor and an associate of Paul; and the fourth Gospel by John, the son of Zebedee. Critical scholarship has challenged all these assertions, but in recent years a tendency is evident to return to the traditional views on the authorship of the four Gospels.

One of the earliest church fathers who lived at the end of the first century refers to the existence of an oral gospel. Eusebius in a quotation from Papias' "Interpretation of our Lord's Declarations" states in effect that the Gospel content was handed down by the living voice. At the end of the first century A.D. only a few disciples were living whom Papias could have consulted, but he declared that he preferred the apostolic preaching as it was delivered orally. Irrespective of Papias' judgment, it substantiates the belief that the gospel message was transmitted orally also. At least for two generations the contents of the apostolic message was proclaimed orally.

Luke provides New Testament readers with a clue as to how the oral tradition was put into writing. He explains in the opening chapter of his Gospel what motivated him to compose his Gospel (Luke 1:1–4), namely, to confirm in writing facts that Theophilus had learned orally. Luke spoke of facts which were taken for granted among Christians, and alluded to the existence of numerous attempts to arrange them in orderly narratives. Luke employs the word "narrative" (Greek *diegesis*) which means an extended account of the life of Christ available but not altogether satisfactory. His prologue permits the inference that the other "gospels" were incomplete in content and drawn from secondary sources, or that they may have been poorly organized without a central theme and thus did not furnish enough biographical material to provide an adequate understanding of Jesus.

By contrast Luke claimed that he had obtained his data from those "who from the beginning were eye-witnesses and ministers of the word" (1:2). Those from whom Luke obtained his facts were not only participants in the information they gave him, but were also personally affected by it and had become disciples of Christ. Luke investigated the facts given him by the informants so that he might produce an orderly and accurate account of the record of Christ's life and sayings.

The fourth evangelist, John, informs his readers that he committed the Gospel to writing so that a reading of it might produce faith in Christ as the Son of God and that by believing in Jesus men might have eternal life (20:31). John did not give an exhaustive life of Jesus but presupposed that his readers would be acquainted with the main facts concerning Him. John was selective in the material that he incorporated in the twenty-one chapters that comprise the Gospel which was probably written around 95 A.D.

Although the Gospels of Mark and Matthew are not quite as definite in furnishing the reader information regarding their origin and reasons for writing them, from statements made in these two Gospels their purposes can be determined. Thus Matthew begins with the asseveration: "The book of the generation of Jesus Christ, the son of David, the son of Abraham" (Matt. 1:1), which duplicates the wording of Gen. 5:1 and thus sets forth the idea that the author wishes to give an important chapter in the history of God's people. Mark's opening statement reads: "The beginning of the gospel of Jesus Christ, the Son of God." This constitutes a title and indicates that what follows is a summary of current preaching and teaching. The purpose, therefore, of the written Gospels was to put into permanent form for posterity what before their inscripturation had been in the minds of the first witnesses of the gospel of Jesus Christ.

The native language of Christ was Palestinian Aramaic. There are Aramaisms in the Gospels, such as Ephphatha (Mark 7:34), Talitha cumi (Mark 5:41), and the cry from the cross, Eloi, Eloi, lama, sabachthani (Mark 15:34). Controversy has been rife whether or not the four Gospels were composed in Greek or Aramaic. Eusebius has quoted a statement by Papias that Matthew composed his history in the Hebrew dialect and that everybody translated it as he was able.[1] How these words of Papias' quotation are to be understood have puzzled students. Did Matthew write his Gospel in Hebrew or Aramaic? Papias does not make clear whether Matthew simply collected notes which were then used by the other evangelists for their gospels, or whether he wrote a narrative that was rendered into other languages. Papias seems to support the idea that before the Gentile church wrote Greek literature, a group of writings in Hebrew or Aramaic existed.

The experiences of the apostolic company plus the forms of preaching and teaching current in the apostolic church were the materials incorporated into the four Gospels. Both

139

the prologue of Luke's Gospel and that the statement of John 20:30–31 guarantee the accuracy of the facts and speeches that are recorded in the eighty-nine chapters that comprise the four Gospels. These four books were authorized by men who were a part of a growing and expanding church. They were not written primarily as literary efforts but essentially to produce faith in the readers. Matthew purported to show his readers that Jesus of Nazareth was the promised Messiah. Mark portrayed Jesus as a man of action and deeds, a presentation he hoped would impress the Romans. Luke was especially concerned about depicting Christ as the universal Savior, employing a smooth style and a wide variety of parables to enlist the interest of cultured people in the Roman Empire. John made use of episodes and sayings of Jesus that had not been employed and recorded by the Synoptic writers (Matthew, Mark and Luke).

The place and time of the public literary promulgation of these four Gospels is lost in obscurity. The earliest quotations from them are found in the writings of Ignatius in the *Epistle of Barnabas, the Teaching of the Twelve Apostles,* and *The Epistle of Polycarp.* The home of these writings was Antioch in Syria. The quotations in these apostolic fathers seem closely identifiable with Matthew's Gospel. If Matthew was written in Hebrew or Aramaic, in Jerusalem, it is possible that it became the basis for the Greek New Testament text used in Antioch where Greek was spoken. The original version could have been available around 50 A.D. in Jerusalem and therefore in existence before the destruction of Jerusalem in 70 A.D.

Regarding the authorship of the Gospel of Mark, Clement of Alexandria wrote: "When Peter had proclaimed the word publicly at Rome, and declared the gospel under the influence of the Spirit; as there was a great number present, they requested Mark, who had followed him from afar, and remembered well what he had said, to reduce these things in writing, and that after composing the gospel he gave it to those who requested it of him. Which, when Peter understood, he directly neither hindered nor encouraged it."[2] Ireneus, a contemporary of Clement also related this tradition around 100 A.D. stating that Peter's preaching was handed down by Mark. If Ireneus' assertion is correct, it would be possible to place the second Gospel, representing Peter's Gospel, around 65 A.D.

The Gospel of Luke may have at first been a private writing directed to Theophilus, a friend of Luke, who may have been a member of the aristocracy. The two volumes that Luke penned were designed to remove any doubts about Christ and the church Jesus had come to establish. Luke's Gospel must have preceded the book of Acts, which was a sequel to the Gospel, and the former could have been in existence by 62 A.D.

John's Gospel had been placed as early as 60 A.D. by the outstanding scholar F. W. Albright. It seems that the last chapter of John was written to refute the rumor that John would never die. This rumor would have had no basis unless John had reached an advanced age. Most conservative scholars assign a date around 85 A.D. to the fourth Gospel.

The Synoptic Problem

Matthew, Mark and Luke have been called the Synoptic Gospels because they have a similar structure regarding the earthly ministry of Christ, and a similar view of His teachings and career. The interesting agreements among the first three Gospels has led to speculation whether their relationships can be traced to a common source. Most of Mark's Gospel can be found in the Gospels of Matthew and Luke, but Matthew and Luke have material not found in Mark. Nevertheless each Gospel has a different emphasis.

The problems raised by these relationships have been stated by Tenney as follows: "If three Gospels are absolutely independent of each other how can one account for the minute verbal agreement in their text? If they are copied from each other, or compiled freely from common sources, how can they be original and authoritative? Are they, then, truly the product of inspired writers, or are they merely combinations of anecdotes which may or may not be true?"[3]

Many theories have been advanced to account for the similarities as well as the dissimilarities found in the Synoptic writings. The most popular theory is the Two Source Hypothesis which claims that Mark was the basis from which Matthew and Luke procured their main outline. Another hypothetical document called "Q" (meaning in German *Quelle*) is alleged to have been used by both Luke and Matthew for the material not obtained from Mark. Canon B. H. Streeter, in *The Four Gospels*, expanded the two source theory into a Four Source Hypothesis by suggesting that Matthew in addition to Mark and "Q" used a special source he called "M," while Luke in addition to Mark and "Q" employed a special source called "L."

While these theories have seemingly answered the problem of the verbal similarities, scholars have not found either the two source or the four source theories satisfactory. The source "Q" has never been found nor is there a reference to its existence in the literature of the church. "Q" is said to have a resemblance to the extant collection "Sayings of Jesus," which has been dated as coming from the second or third century A.D. This collection is assigned to the Gnostics and is dependent on oral tradition and thus must be considered a secondary source.

Dissatisfaction with the Two Source Hypothesis has led to a new approach to the Synoptic problem. A new type of literary criticism known as form criticism has come into vogue. This new approach endeavors to assay the written Gospels by trying to determine the history of the individual Gospels. Proponents of *Formgeschichte* (a German word meaning literally history of forms) believe that the Gospels are comprised of different literary types or genres. Form criticism endeavors to study the literary form of documents that are purported to preserve earlier traditions. Filson claims that "its basic assumption is that the earlier oral use of the tradition shaped the material and resulted in the variety of literary forms found in the final written record."[4]

Form criticism, used first in the Old Testament field, was adopted by K.L. Schmidt (1919), M. Dibelius (1919), and R. Bultmann (1921). Ideas and principles found in Olrik's studies of folklore, Gunkel's identification of oral traditions in the Old Testament, Wellhausen's critical attention to individual items of the gospel tradition and Norden's study of prose style and mission discourses were the inspiration for development and adoption of form criticism. The interest in form criticism was especially fostered by the fact that between Christ's preaching and the composition of the four Gospels there was an oral period. In addition, an attempt was also made to determine what part the early church had in transmitting the gospel.

Form criticism emphasizes the following as presuppositions of its methodology: 1) The Gospels in our present manuscripts are not single creations out of a whole cloth but consist of collections of material, the final selection and arrangement of which we owe to the evangelists themselves. 2) The present Gospels have a prehistory in terms of oral transmission. Small collections or related materials are supposed to have been circulated in the early church where

143

they were used for preaching or catechetical instruction. 3) The small oral tradition units were classified as follows: pronouncement stories, miracle stories, and sayings (subdivided as wisdom words, parables, myths, legends). The various form-critical scholars are by no means agreed as to these classifications. The form critics seek to remove the original form of the story or saying by stripping it of its traditional accretions and of the alleged editorial additions made by the evangelists. Following this procedure the form critic seeks to establish the *Sitz-im-Leben* (the life situation) of a pericope: trying to determine for what purpose, or to meet what need, did the first church preserve, shape, or invent this or that story or saying.

It was concluded by the earliest practitioners of form criticism that the earlier the form the simpler was the nature of the earliest narratives. Schmidt was not able to break them down into smaller units according to the methodology he had adopted, so the Passion and Easter accounts were not treated as recording what actually happened, but were interpreted as having been created and influenced by the Easter faith of the early church.

Form criticism as already related had its origin because critics believed that the old source hypotheses were inadequate. The same critics also questioned the historical reliability of Mark, alleged to have been the first Gospel. Form criticism which aims at examining the oral gospel assumes that the various forms were creations of the Christian community. If this assumption is correct it would mean that the Gospels tell us more about the church that created the various forms of literary genre in the Gospels, than they tell us about the sayings and deeds of Jesus. Form critics believe that by examining the origin of the different types of literary genre they can determine the occasion for their origin. In the light of this analysis, critics then proceed to determine the nature, the historicity and reliability of the gospel material.

Two big questions are asked by form critics: What in the Gospels was uttered by Jesus? What sayings did the early church place into the mouth of Jesus? Form criticism will examine a saying, a miracle, a parable, or any one of the other types of material found by them and then question whether or not Jesus really said or did that which is attributed to Him by the evangelists.

Rudolph Bultmann was one of the main proponents of form criticism. Each of the great form critics has his own emphasis and point of view to promote. Bultmann depended on history to interpret the Gospel forms. However Bultmann's methodology in essence amounts to another form of historical criticism. Bultmann has dissolved the Christian faith in the acids of demythologizing. This position has been strikingly presented in a parody of the Apostle's Creed which reads as follows:

Bultmann believes in Jesus Christ, *not* the only Son of God, (yet) our Lord; who was *not* conceived by the Holy Ghost, *not* born of the Virgin Mary, suffered under Pontius Pilate; was crucified, dead and buried; he did *not* descend into hell; the third day he is (thought to have) risen from the dead; he did *not* ascend into heaven; and sitteth *not* at the right hand of God the Father Almighty; from thence he shall *not* come to judge the quick and the dead.[5]

---

[5]From *Tradition and Interpretation in Matthew,* by Günther Bornkam, Gerhard Barth, and Heinz Joachim Held. Published in the U.S.A. by the Westminster Press, 1963, p.55. Copyright © SCM Press, Ltd., 1963. Used by permission.

Form criticism has dealt essentially with the Synoptic Gospels. The Johannine Gospel, it is claimed, is plainly the work of an outstanding personality and is regarded by critical scholars as the product of tradition.

Redaction Criticism
History has shown that the type of literary criticism that was developed by scholars who were influenced by theological liberalism, was found unsatisfactory to a generation of scholars that appeared in the theological arena after the conclusion of World War I. Dissatisfaction with the conclusions of literary Gospel criticism spawned form criticism. The latter has now been weighed in the scales of critical evaluation and been found wanting. Out of form criticism has now come redaction criticism. While form criticism was a major development after World War I, redaction criticism was a product after World War II. Nor is it envisioned that redaction criticism will be the final development in the critical approach to the New Testament.

The leaders of redaction criticism are the German New Testament scholars Günther Bornkamm, Hans Conzelmann, and Willie Marxsen. Each of these advocators of redaction criticism is developing a school of followers. These three German scholars have developed their critical views in connection with Matthew, Luke and Mark respectively. Thus Bornkamm, in his book *Tradition and Interpretation in Matthew* averred: "Matthew is not only a hander-on of the narrative, but also its oldest exegete, and in fact the first to interpret the journey of the disciples with Jesus in the storm and the stilling of the storm with reference to discipleship and that means with reference to the little ship of the church."[5] Bornkamm claims that Matthew has changed the tradition as he received it and this

146

shows the modern student that Matthew hereby was creating theology in the interest of his evangelical purpose, and developing his understanding of the church in view of the parousia (the Second Coming). Bornkamm believes Matthew has a peculiar view of the meaning of the Jewish law and its role in the Christian faith.

Hans Conzelmann in his *Theology of St. Luke* has portrayed St. Luke not as an historian but as a theologian. This is quite a different position from that taken by both C. K. Barrett and A. T. Robertson who wrote books setting forth Luke as a reputable and reliable historian. Conzelmann, by contrast, contends that Luke was not interested in historical accuracy but that he determined facts to suit his theological purpose and his understanding of *Heilsgeschichte* (salvation history). Conzelmann did not hesitate to supply the smallest details of Christ's life, even though they did not have any foundation in fact. Conzelmann claims that the order of events in Luke is imaginary and that history was manufactured by Luke in the interest of his theology.

Willi Marxsen has done redactional studies in Mark, as may be seen from a study of his book, *The Evangelist Mark* (1956, in German). Marxsen proposed three separate "settings of life" for the Synoptic tradition. He argued that if one believes that it is necessary to consider a life setting for the parables in the life of Jesus and for other types of literary genre in the Synoptic tradition, then as form critics contend, one must also uncover a setting in the life of the church for the creation and transmission of the tradition. So it also follows that there must be a consideration of the setting and purpose of the evangelist.

One of the major outcomes of form criticism has been the third quest for the historical Jesus. The liberal quest of the nineteenth century had ended in a dead end. All the first quest's literary and historical work, the source analysis and psychological investigation had ended in producing a picture of the life of Christ that was not true to the facts. Form criticism produced the conclusion that very little might be known of Jesus of Nazareth. The second quest did not satisfy many followers of Bultmann who consequently embarked on the third quest. Ernst Käsemann was one of the main New Testament scholars to pursue "the new quest." According to Käsemann, the Gospels cannot present us with the bare facts of history as modern historiography does. This is impossible because New Testament documents show a diversity of interpretation of the historical facts about Jesus. Käsemann therefore believed that the historical Jesus was to be discovered in the *kerygma*, in the proclamation.

According to Professor Perrin, redaction criticism has not only serious implications for the life of Jesus research but also for the way the Gospel narratives were to be understood. Perrin claims, "but it is when we come to redaction criticism that the whole matter comes to a head. For redaction criticism not only makes life of Jesus research very difficult, it also raises fundamental questions with regard to the vitality of a life of Jesus theology."[6]

Even critical scholars have been skeptical of form criticism as a viable and legitimate interpretative methodology. Form critics are unable to assign all the gospel material to different literary genre by this method. Furthermore form criticism fails to consider the part played by eyewitnesses in accurately passing on historical data. Nor does it do justice to the historical sense, intelligence and integrity of the early Christian followers. While the topical principle is used in certain of the Gospels, it does not take into account the chronological structure of Christ's life; in fact, form criti-

148

cism discredits most of it. The assumption that there was an oral period in the transmission of the gospel that probably lasted no longer than twenty years is true. During this time the good news was proclaimed by men who had been with Jesus and who had received the Great Commission from Him, and any false reports by the proclaimers of the gospel could have been corrected by those who had personally known Jesus. Filson also finds fault with form criticism because, "The tendency to assume radical distortion of the tradition in the Hellenistic church is refuted by the prevailingly Semitic character of the common Synoptic tradition; and its results are warped by unexamined assumptions, such as the miracle stories are largely late creations, and that explicit Christology arose first in the church rather than in the mind of Jesus."[7]

All forms of higher criticism, source, form and redaction criticism, have been and are approaches which have questioned the reliability of the facts reported in the Gospels. These types of criticism all assumed that the Gospels were not inspired writings in which the Holy Spirit had caused the author to record reliable facts and interpretations about the life of Jesus. The Gospels are important in theology because they establish Christ as the Son of God and Redeemer of men. If the conclusions of source, form and redaction critics are valid and acceptable, it would mean undermining one of the most important areas of Christian theology, namely, that of Christology, that locus of the Christian faith that deals with the person, work, and mission of Jesus Christ. Is the church's Christology built upon what Jesus taught and did or is it based on what the early church claimed He said and did? The difference is tremendous! Christianity cannot survive if the conclusions of the critics are accepted and promulgated.

149

11
Letters as Literature

The majority of writings in the New Testament belong to the epistolary genre. Of the twenty-seven books comprising the New Testament canon, twenty-one may be classified as epistles or letters.

The epistles, according to the custom of the time, have an introduction in which are found the name of the writer and that of the addressee, either a person or a church. This is followed by a greeting, the body of the letter, a conclusion, and concluding greeting. Hebrews, James and I John deviate from this pattern. Some specific occasion usually prompted the penning of an epistle and the life situation can readily be inferred from it. The writing of the epistles was caused either by personal motives due to the author's initiative (Philemon, II John), or they were written in reply to questions addressed to the apostle (I Cor. 1:11; II Cor. 7:5-7; I Thess. 3:5,6). Paul requested that a letter sent by him to one congregation should be read not only by this one congregation but by others as well, regarding his teachings and their conforming to them. Both Peter and Paul stated that their letters were the Word of God (I Thess. 2:13; I Pet. 1:12).

The majority of New Testament epistles were written by apostles or in a few instances by individuals who knew the apostles and whose writings received apostolic sanction. The letters or epistles addressed to the churches dealt with doctrinal and practical matters. Even those epistles addressed to individuals contain matters of great importance applicable to Christians in general and not necessarily confined to one person or church.

Paul addressed the following letters to congregations: I and II Corinthians, Romans, Galatians, Ephesians, Philippians, Colossians, and I and II Thessalonians; and the following to individuals: I and II Timothy, Titus and Philemon. Of the Pauline letters addressed to churches, Corinthians, Galatians, Philippians and Thessalonians contain the most personal elements, Romans has fewer, and Ephesians and Colossians have the least. Galatians and Ephesians are composed on a rhetorical plan and have considerable rhetorical elements. In the pastoral letters numerous personal references are made and contain few rhetorical elements. The letter to Philemon was regarded by Deissmann as the most personal of the Pauline letters, although it also contains rhetorical elements.

The Critical Historical Treatment of the Pauline Corpus
Albert Schweitzer in his *Paul and His Interpreters* has traced the development of the critical studies regarding the Pauline letters since the days of the Reformation. Schweitzer claims that orthodox believers used the Pauline epistles primarily as proof texts, and that their interpretation was to establish dogma. In the eighteenth century the pietists and the rationalists reacted to this procedure, each in their own way, and they employed the Pauline corpus to

151

foster their objectives. J. S. Semler and J. D. Michaelis, early proponents of historical criticism, used various Pauline letters to set forth their new views. Semler in his *Paraphrases of Romans and First Corinthians* emphasized the fact that these Pauline letters were temporarily conditioned letters in which the purely cultural elements must be distinguished from what is of an abiding value. Semler also argued that the epistles had the form of a "church liturgy," and thus at one time may have had a different form. He also contrasted the non-Jewish and Jewish thought within the Pauline letters. Romans 15 and 16 and II Cor. 11, 12; 13:14, were separated from the letters in which they were found.

The Tübingen School and the Pauline Epistles

In the nineteenth century some severe attacks were made upon the integrity and authenticity of a number of the Pauline letters. According to the critics, that was the century that freed interpretation from the shackles of dogma. In the writings of J. E. C. Schmidt new tendencies appear which question the authenticity of I Timothy and II Thessalonians on literary grounds. The two German scholars, Eichhorn and DeWette, assailed the Pauline authorship of I Timothy and Titus. F. C. Bauer also continued his attack upon Paul's letters and his criticism eventually ascribed only five letters to Paul. Bauer considered only five of the twenty-seven New Testament books as apostolic. In his book, *Symbolik and Mythologie*, Bauer set forth his major ideas and asserted that "without philosophy, history seems dumb and dead." He applied Hegel's dialectical principles to New Testament writings. All historical movements were viewed by Bauer in terms of a series of historical advances by means of thesis (advance) and antithesis (reaction) resulting in a synthesis (a new thesis). He postu-

152

lated a conflict between Paul and Peter on the basis of I Cor. 1:12, and as a result of this supposed clash a new thesis, Catholic Christianity, was established. All New Testament writings that reflected either the Pauline or Petrine position were therefore considered late second century documents. In the area of New Testament criticism the dominant school became that of the Tübingen scholars. Another namesake, Bruno Bauer, went so far as to question the integrity and authenticity of all Pauline writings and he thus adopted a completely skeptical position. He claimed that the book of Acts does not include knowledge of the Pauline letters and contended that Paul was more primitive than the letters ascribed to him. He further taught that Paulinism was nothing but the Hellenization of Christianity.

The views of both Bauers were immediately attacked by conservative scholars. J. C. K. von Hofmann and many Lutherans defended the authenticity of the Pauline Epistles. The citation of Paul in I Clement (A.D. 95) and Ignatius (A.D. 110) and the omission of the anti-Jewish feelings in the postapostolic writings were cited against the theories of the Tübingen School. Liberal scholars also attacked the Hegelian interpretation of Paul by F. C. Bauer. Followers of Schleiermacher and A. Ritschl repudiated the alleged hostility between Paul and Peter. By those nineteenth century followers of Bauer, as for example, Pfleiderer, a revision was adopted of the genuine letters of Paul. Apart from the pastorals only Ephesians and II Thessalonians were questioned.

Ellis claims that even though Bauer's philosophical presuppositions were wrong and his understanding of New Testament literature was completely erroneous, he still rendered a service to New Testament studies by introducing an inductive approach to the study of Pauline literature. Bauer also brought into clear relief some of the problems dealing with the apostolic age that later were to occupy scholars. What was the relationship between Jesus and Paul? Did Jewish and Hellenistic thought affect Christianity? What are the proper philosophies that undergird the study of Christian origins?

In America in the nineteenth century the Tübingen school was not accepted although scholars like B. W. Bacon and A. C. McGiffert rejected I and II Timothy and Titus as Pauline. However, in Great Britain J. B. Lightfoot accepted the Pauline authorship of the pastoral letters. British scholars by the application of sound historical interpretation affected the future of Pauline studies in the English-speaking world. Sir William Ramsey's espousal of the Lucan authorship of Acts exerted a great influence on subsequent British Pauline studies. Ramsey engaged in archaeological and historical research in Asia Minor and subsequently defended the historical accuracy of the New Testament. His reconstruction of Acts in relationship to Paul's epistles also greatly influenced New Testament studies.

In the twentieth century, literary criticism of the Pauline writings and Acts has centered in (a) continuing efforts to reconstruct the life and letters of Paul; (b) the publication of Paul's genuine letters; (c) the dates and places of origin of the Pauline Letters; (d) the authorship of the various epistles; and (e) questions relative to individual epistles.

Despite the repudiation of the Tübingen school's historical reconstruction, some of its views have continued to be maintained and Bauer's influence is still evident in this century. While the Tübingen's original formula of thesis, antithesis and synthesis has been modified, yet many scholars today manifest the effects of this nineteenth century school of criticism. Thus Fuller has written: "Yet most of our standard guides to the study of Paul—Dibelius, Lietzmann, A. D. Nock and W. L. Knox for instance are, we are surprised to learn, still committed basically to the Tübingen view. The ghost of Bauer is far from dead."[1] J. Munck in his book *Paul and the Salvation of Mankind* has given a very effective repudiation of Bauer's position as espoused today. Munck asserts that the sole issue between Peter and Paul was their respective understanding of redemptive history. The Judaizers in the Galatian churches were not emissaries from James but were troublemakers in the local churches. According to Munck, Paul's main difference with the Jerusalem apostles was regarding the question of whether or not the Gentiles should have first received the gospel. It was Paul's contention that he should bring the gospel to the Gentiles. Munck maintains that the difference between Paul and the Jerusalem church concerned itself with the priority of whether the Gentiles or the Jews were intended to be the first recipients of the gospel. Paul argued for the priority of the Gentiles. Ellis believes that Munck's views do not ignore the critical emphases but that they pave the way for a constructive advance in Pauline studies.

The Time of the Origin of the Pauline Epistles
Among scholars different theories are propounded regarding the time of the origin and the place of composition of the Pauline Epistles. According to the older view, Galatians was written in 57 A.D., or as Lightfoot said in his introduction to his Galatian commentary, "some place must be found for the Galatian Epistle in the group which comprises the Epistles to the Corinthians and Romans, but such coincidences come far short of being proof that the two epistles were written about the same time. To write about

155

the topic of justification and other topics would be appropriate at any time."[2] In the opinion of many scholars a good case has been made for the South Galatian theory which holds that the Galatian Epistle was written in 48 A.D. and that it was sent to the congregations in the southern part of Galatia.

In the course of his first and second missionary journeys Paul wrote the two Thessalonian Epistles; the first in 51 A.D. from Corinth; the second in 52 A.D. from Corinth also. In the course of his third missionary journey Paul penned I and II Corinthians and Romans. During this journey Paul spent three years in Ephesus (53–56 A.D.) from where he wrote I Corinthians probably in 55 A.D. (I Cor. 16:8). Somewhere in Macedonia he probably wrote II Corinthians, possibly in 56 A.D. (II Cor. 7:5). In the year 57 A.D. when Paul was in Corinth as a guest of Gaius (Rom. 16:23), he wrote Romans.

The letters to the Ephesians, Philippians, Colossians and Philemon were written while Paul was a prisoner. Where and when were these four inspired epistles written? Paul was a prisoner in Caesarea, Ephesus and Rome. Only a few scholars have held that the captivity letters were written from Caesarea between 58–60 A.D. The Roman theory has had many advocates in the past and still has to this day. These letters are believed to have been penned between 60–62 A.D. Duncan, however, has proposed a theory that designates Ephesus as the place from which these epistles originated while Paul was a prisoner between 53–56 A.D. Depending on how the evidence appeals to a biblical scholar, this will determine his views on the date and place of origin of Paul's imprisonment letters.

The last group of epistles written by Paul were I and II Timothy and Titus. Critical New Testament scholars have denied Paul as the author of these letters. Harrison, in *The Problem of the Pastoral Epistles* (1920), on grounds of their second century vocabulary and style, rejected the traditional view of the release and the second Roman captivity tradition, and he placed I Timothy and Titus and II Timothy in that order. Harrison has found in these three letters, five genuine Pauline fragments of which he calls II Timothy and Titus amplifications. I Timothy is attributed to Paul. Dibelius has placed the pastoral epistles into the ecclesiastical struggles of the postapostolic period and related them to the *Didache*, Isocrates and Pseudo-Isocrates.

The prima facie evidence of the Pastorals themselves supports Paul as the writer since his name appears at the beginning of each letter. The autobiographical references in the Pastoral epistles coincide with the life of Paul between his release from his first Roman imprisonment and his death in 67 A.D.

The basic style of evidence regarding the genuineness of documents was stated many years ago by Simon Greenleaf, who wrote:

Every document, apparently ancient, coming from the proper repository or custody, and bearing on its face no evident marks of forgery, the law presumes to be genuine, and devolves on the opposing part of the burden of proving it otherwise.[3]

The early church always accepted the Pastoral letters as Pauline. What are the reasons for questioning Paul's authorship of these letters despite their direct testimony? The arguments advanced against their genuineness are: 1. The language and style are not Pauline; 2. Opposition of the epistles to second century gnosticism; 3. Discrepancies between Acts and the pastorals—Acts relates only one Roman imprisonment at the end of which Paul was put to death; 4. The type of ecclesiastical organization is too advanced for the first Christian century.

All of these negative objections have been satisfactorily answered by the defenders of the Pauline tradition and held by the early church. There is good reason to believe that Paul was released after his first imprisonment. The tradition regarding his journey to Rome is early and undisputed. Assuming Paul's release, the years between 61 and his death, Paul would have had sufficient time for the activities mentioned in the three Pastoral epistles. The personal references to Paul are so true to life that it is difficult to conceive of a forger having created them and then being able to convince the early church that these three letters were genuine Pauline correspondence, if this were not the case. In answer to the objection that the church organization is too advanced, it is to be noted that Paul had already appointed elders on his first missionary journey. In Eph. 4:11 he speaks of pastors and teachers and in Phil. 1:1 of deacons. The organization in the Pastorals actually is not elaborate nor more advanced than the type set forth in other Pauline letters.

Relative to the heresies that are attacked in the Pastorals, it should be noted that the errorists do have some characteristics of Gnosticism which had its beginning long before the second century; but most of the heresies have a strong Judaic coloring which is not characteristic of second century Gnosticism. The style of Paul's letters differs in each epistle and often times even within the epistle itself. Some scholars believe that the vocabulary presents the greatest difficulty for supporting the Pauline authorship of the Pastorals. Of the 848 word vocabulary, 306 words or more than thirty-six percent are not found in any other of the

Pauline letters. In answer to this objection it should be noted that the large percentage of new words may in part be due to the new subject matter introduced in the Pastorals. Critics of the Pauline authorship claim that the great change in vocabulary occurs in connection with the little words, connectives and prepositions. How can this fact be explained? Paul's vocabulary often changes just as radically in the accepted epistles as in Titus and the two Timothy letters. The fact is that Paul quotes numerous "faithful sayings" of the church. It must be remembered that Paul spoke and wrote Greek as his second language which he learned mostly from association. In coming to Rome and remaining there for some years, he has been introduced to a new kind of Greek, influenced by Latin. This is confirmed by the fact that "new words" are found with much greater frequency in those apostolic fathers connected with Rome (i.e. Clement, Hermas, Tatian, Justin) than in the non-Roman fathers. Some of the "new words" also belong to the literary vocabulary of the *Koine*. This may be due to Paul's association with Luke during the years that the epistles of Titus, and I and II Timothy were composed.

There is, therefore, no conclusive evidence to overthrow the internal testimony in the pastoral letters that Paul is their author. The critical objections make the Pastorals pseudonymous writings, a situation that would be out of character with the concept of biblical inspiration inasmuch as these letters as part of the New Testament, are inspired by God.

Professor E. J. Goodspeed attempted to deal with the question regarding which letters belonged to the Pauline corpus. The Chicago professor departed from earlier authorities as did Harnack and his predecessors. Goodspeed put forth the theory that around the year 90 A.D. an admirer of Paul published in Ephesus the Epistles of Paul (with the exception of the Pastorals) and wrote the letter to the Ephesians as the introduction to the Pauline collection. John Knox took the theory one step farther and proposed that it was Onesimus who published the Epistle to Philemon. According to C. L. Mitton, a number of scholars have been won over to this hypothesis. In opposition to this theory other scholars offer the following criticisms: 1. The text of Ephesians requires some addressee, and such a primitive omission leads to the conclusion that the letter was a circular one; 2. In no ancient manuscript does Ephesians ever begin or end the Pauline collection; 3. It would be difficult to consider the content of Ephesians as a summary of non-Pauline thinking; 4. While there may have been a pre-Pauline collection that was assembled, Goodspeed's and Knox's theories are objectionable from the point of view of rejecting the clear testimony of the text and reinterpreting its meaning. All theories that reject the clear statements of the text, especially when no textual problems exist in the manuscripts, call into question the reliability of the scriptural text, and are incompatible with the truthful character of the documents themselves.

The General Epistles
The General or Catholic Epistles are usually classed as: James, Hebrews, I and II Peter, I, II, III John and Jude. They are so designated because they apparently were directed to several communities or to the Christian church at large rather than to any one person or congregation. It would be a mistake to consider them a unified group since each epistle has its own individual purpose and message. Scholars have differed as to which of these seven epistles should be grouped together. Some consider only James, II

160

Peter and I John as warranting the title of General Epistles. Other scholars add one of the following: I Peter, Jude, II and III John to this classification.

The Epistle of James is written by James, a servant of Jesus Christ. Conservative biblical scholarship has identified this James either with the Apostle James, the son of Zebedee, or with James of Jerusalem, the brother of Christ. Critical scholarship has proposed the idea that the epistle, written to Jewish Christians, had as one of its purposes an attack on the Pauline doctrine of justification by faith. This reason together with the author's acquaintance with the Greek language and his manner of speaking is believed to suggest a date around 96–100 A.D. This late dating, however, is based on some false assumptions. The alleged disagreement between Paul and James on justification by works versus justification by faith is only an apparent contradiction. In Romans 4 and Galatians 3, Paul is describing the manner of becoming justified before God. Man cannot earn his justification but is justified when he believes in the vicarious death of Christ on Calvary's cross for his sins. This belief is created by faith and results in man being declared righteous. When, however, an individual is justified by faith, a gift of the Holy Spirit, this faith manifests itself by good deeds. Good works consequently are evidence that a person who claims to be a Christian really has saving faith. As James has said: "Faith without works is dead." The supposition that if a Christian believed in the Pauline doctrine of justification by faith it did not matter how he lived, is being denounced and warned against by James. The great New Testament scholar Zahn contended that James was either the first letter written or that it was penned sometime during the sixties prior to the destruction of Jerusalem.

161

How Dependable Is the Bible?

The two letters, I and II Peter, attributed by their contents to the Apostle Peter are generally denied to be Petrine by critical scholarship. While I Peter is considered of relatively small value as a source of doctrine, it "is one of the most beautiful writings in the New Testament, not philosophical or profound, but full of the purest spirit of devotion." Critical scholarship has rejected this Petrine letter on the following grounds: 1. The correct and elegant Greek could not have been written by a Galilean fisherman; 2. The epistle is saturated with Pauline teachings which Peter could not have known or accepted; 3. The date for writing this letter would not be in harmony with the date of Peter's martyrdom about 67 A.D. These arguments are insufficient to overthrow the clear testimony of the epistle. Both internal and external evidences support the Petrine authorship. No other New Testament letter has a better attestation. II Pet. 3:1 has the earliest acknowledgment of the authenticity of I Peter. The epistle is alluded to in the Epistle to the Corinthians written by the apostolic fathers, Barnabas and Clement. In I Peter the author is said to be Peter and in 5:1 he claims to have been an eyewitness to the sufferings of Jesus. There is a similarity between Peter's speeches in Acts and his words in I Peter (compare Acts 10:34 with I Pet. 1:17; Acts 2:32–36; Acts 10:40–41 with I Pet. 1:21; Acts 4:10,11 with I Pet. 2:7,8).

The Second Epistle of Peter is also considered by critical scholars to be an anonymous letter and the last written book in the New Testament despite the first verse clearly stating that its author was "Simon Peter, a servant and an apostle of Jesus Christ." Critical scholars claim: 1. That the anonymous author attached the Apostle's name to lend authority; 2. The author of I Peter was not the author of II Peter; 3. The date the "letter" was written is very late and should be

162

placed somewhere between 125–150 A.D. This late post-apostolic date, it is assumed, is supported by the following facts: 1. II Peter incorporates Jude 2:2–17 with II Peter borrowing from Jude; 2. In II Pet. 3:4 mention is made of the "death of the fathers," who are identified with the early church leaders; 3. II Peter refers to the epistles of Paul as "Scriptures" (3:15–16), a term only applied to the Old Testament Scriptures in the Apostolic Age.

Pseudonymity is certainly a concept not in harmony with truthfulness. The Epistle of II Peter presents itself as a genuine production of the Apostle Peter who claims that he was an eyewitness at the transfiguration of Christ (1:16–18) and was warned of his impending death by our Lord (1:14). While it is true some differences in style exist between the two books, yet striking likenesses between I and II Peter are also evident as has been pointed out by the New Testament scholar Zahn. If II Peter is a forgery, no doubt the forger would have attempted to imitate the style and language of I Peter! Peter's reference to Paul's epistles does not necessarily mean that all of Paul's letters had already been collected but is an allusion to those letters with which Peter was acquainted. It is mere conjecture to assume that II Peter is dealing with a more advanced stage of apostasy than that evidenced in Peter's lifetime.

The Epistle of Jude

This one-chapter book is assigned by critical scholarship to the period between 125–150 A.D., the postapostolic period of church history, and it is said to have been written from Rome to Christians everywhere as an attack upon gnostic doctrine and antinomian morality.

The critical position rejects the clear statement of the text about its authorship. According to the book's own tes-

timony, it was written by "Jude, a servant of Jesus Christ
and brother of James." Since James was one of the brothers
of Jesus, Jude was likewise one of his brethren. Matt. 13:55
and Mark 6:3 indicate that Jesus had a brother by that
name. Because the term "apostle" is not used in verse
one, Jude is excluded as being one of the twelve Apostles.
Since the general character of the letter does not disclose
the exact time of writing nor its place of origin, Zahn has
placed it around 75 A.D., but any time from 66 A.D. to 75–80
A.D. is considered acceptable.

12
St. John's Writings in the Face of Criticism

In his argument to the fourth Gospel John Calvin wrote: "I am accustomed to call this Gospel the key which opens the door to the understanding of the others." The Gospel of John is especially significant because about fifty percent of its chapters give the very words of Jesus.

Yet this Gospel has been called into question because of its differences from the others. While there are differences, it is nevertheless true that if the reader takes the fourth Gospel on its own merits, it is difficult to avoid the conclusion that it was composed either by an eyewitness or else draws upon the reminiscence of an eyewitness.

From the second century until the nineteenth, the Apostle John, the son of Zebedee, was considered the author of five New Testament writings: the fourth Gospel, the three Epistles of John and the Apocalypse or Revelation. In the last one hundred years critical scholarship has rejected the Johannine authorship of all five of these apostolic writings.

How Dependable Is the Bible?

The Gospel of John in the Face of Modern Criticism

Till the nineteenth century, Roman Catholic, Lutheran
and other Protestant scholars had accepted the tradition of
the early church that John was the author of the fourth
Gospel. However, since the early part of the nineteenth
century the Johannine authorship has been questioned; and
to this day, it is a subject of dispute which perennially
becomes a topic for debate. By the year 1900, liberal and
conservative scholars were locked in a hopeless controversy
about the fourth Gospel's authorship, its date of writing, the
historicity of its contents and its real purpose, as well as its
relationship to the Synoptic Gospels.

The oldest reference to the Apostle John as author of the
fourth Gospel is found in the Muratorian Fragment dated
about 170 A.D. Ireneus stated that John, the disciple whom
Jesus loved, published the Gospel of Ephesus. This tradition was accepted by Clement of Alexandria (about 200
A.D.) and by the anti-Marcionite prologue to the Gospel of
John. The Johannine authorship was also accepted by
Ptolemaeus. Papias, who is believed to have been close to
the time of the apostolic tradition, does not mention the
Johannine authorship of the fourth Gospel nor does he
deny it. The Apocryphal Acts of John are silent about the
Gospel of John. In some parts of the church there is
supposed to have been opposition manifested to the apostolic authorship of John, possibly because of the fact that
the Gnostics used this Gospel to support their erroneous
teachings.

At the end of the nineteenth century the Johannine
authorship of the fourth Gospel was widely held both on the
basis of external as well as internal evidence. The classical
statements for the Johannine authorship were formulated
by B. F. Westcott and J. B. Lightfoot. The latter showed that

166

the fourth Gospel was penned by a Palestinian Jew and by a person who must have been an eyewitness of the events described. These two eminent British New Testament scholars claimed that the author was the Apostle John, who in the Gospel is alluded to as the "beloved disciple."

The traditional position of the early Christian church as outlined by Westcott and Lightfoot was rejected by liberal critical scholarship. Critical scholars are just as certain that John the Apostle was not the author, but that the fourth Gospel was the product of Hellenistic mysticism and that it originated in the second century. Arguments against the traditional position were given as follows: 1. The approximate date of 100 A.D. of the Gospel's writing was too late for John the Apostle to have possibly been the author. Some New Testament scholars also assert that the Apostle John was martyred by the Jews much earlier than 90 A.D. thus making it impossible for him to have been the author. 2. Those opposed to the Johannine authorship further claim that there is evidence to the contrary. 3. Christians in the second century are supposed to have been opposed to the fourth Gospel. The Alogi, a Christian sect that rejected the Logos doctrine, ascribed the authorship of the fourth Gospel to the gnostic Cerintheus. Hippolytus of Rome found it necessary to defend John's authorship (about 190–235 A.D.). 4. According to critical scholars, Mark and Luke indicate in their writings that the Disciple John was a Galilean, while the writer of the fourth Gospel, they maintain, lived in or near Jerusalem.

Modern views regarding the authorship of the Gospel of John are various. Some critics have suggested that the Disciple John provided the material for the Gospel and that one of his pupils actually composed it. Another view alleged to have originated in early times was that John the Elder of

167

Ephesus, a prominent layman, was the writer of the fourth Gospel. Yet another modern view proposes that the author of the fourth Gospel will never be known since there is no way of ever determining its authorship. Hence the Gospel is regarded as an anonymous writing. A fourth theory is suggested by those who believe it to be a composite work in which the literary activity of at least two writers can be discerned.

Those scholars who follow the view that John the Elder is the author of the Gospel of John contend that he employed traditions that he had received (i.e. writings of the Synoptists plus a Jerusalem tradition) from John the Apostle and that John the Elder used them as a starting point for independent meditations concerning the meaning of Christ. The distinctive contribution of the real author of John's Gospel is supposed to be reflected in the free compositions of the evangelist. The Gospel of John has as one of its distinctive features statements that begin with "I am." When, for example, Jesus says in this Gospel: "I am the light of the world," or "I am the bread of life," these are not supposed to be sayings of Jesus but the reflections of the writer about the meaning of Jesus. This interpretation was the position of B. H. Streeter in his book *The Four Gospels.*

Recent commentaries by Bultmann, Hoskyns, Dodd and Barrett have rejected the Johannine authorship of the fourth Gospel. Dodd takes the position that the author was some unknown Christian of the second century generation of Christians. Barrett believes that John the Apostle came to Ephesus where he gathered a group of disciples about him. As a man of influence, he fanned the apocalyptic hopes of his followers. After John's death, as envisioned by Barrett, a number of his admirers were motivated to meditate on the meaning of Christian eschatology and wrote the apocalypse around the year 96 A.D. Yet another disciple wrote the three Epistles, with one pupil writing I John, another II John and III John. Still another follower, well read in Judaism and Hellenism, wrote the first twenty chapters of the Gospel. This version was not popular and Barrett speculates that possibly the evangelist died before publishing it. When members of the Gnostic cult saw this version they found material in it that coincided with their speculations. It was only later that the Christian church came to appreciate and correctly evaluate the fourth Gospel, realizing that it did not support Gnosticism but was actually an attack upon this form of philosophical religion. The Gospel of John was then edited and the twenty-first chapter added. The material in this additional chapter may have been left by the evangelist. Actually, the author of the fourth Gospel was the greatest theologian of the early church but his name was forgotten by succeeding generations. However, he had placed in the Gospel references to "the beloved disciple" which allusions were only partially understood.

Conservative New Testament scholarship believes that the following internal evidence definitely points to John, the son of Zebedee, as the author. 1. The writer appears to employ the first person plural (1:14 and perhaps 21:24). 2. That the writer was one of Christ's apostles appears from many minute and detailed references, reflected especially in a description of impressions made on the disciples by events in Christ's life (1:37; 2:11; 4:27, 54; 9:2; 11:8–16; 12:4–6, 21,22; 13:23–26; 18:15; 19:26,27,35; 20:8). 3. The author mentions the disciple whom Jesus loved (chapters 13:23; 19:26; 20:2; 21:7,20,21) and identifies him with the writer of the book in chapter 21:24. Of the twelve Disciples, the fourth Gospel does not mention Matthew, James the son of Alphaeus, Simon Zelotes, and the sons of Zebedee. The first three were not a part of the intimate circle of the Lord to whom the title "beloved disciple" could have been applied. That by inference would leave only James, the son of Zebedee, who died early (Acts 12:3), thus leaving only John. 4. The strongly Aramaic character of the fourth Gospel's writing style would favor a Jew as writer. 5. The author shows an intimate acquaintance with the geography, history and customs of the Jews (cf. 1:21,28,46; 2:6; 3:33; 4:5, 27 RSV; 5:2,3; 7:40–52; 9:7; 10:22,23; 11:18; 18:28; 19:31). The fourth Gospel also gives more details than do the other three Gospels. The internal evidence harmonizes in a unique manner with the tradition of the Johannine authorship.

The Date of the Gospel
The New Testament critical scholarship has differed in its proposals for the time of composition of the fourth Gospel. Radical scholars placed it into the middle of the second century A.D. Such a date, however, is no longer tenable since the discovery of two papyrus fragments. One fragment dated by paleographers as having been written in 125 A.D. contained a few verses from John 18 and thus gives evidence that this Gospel had already been circulating for some time. Inasmuch as the fragment was found in Egypt it furnishes tangible evidence to the early and widespread dissemination of the fourth Gospel. Another fragment dated around 150 A.D. gave incidents from the life of Jesus and uses the fourth Gospel as one of its sources. Therefore, a date for this Gospel of around 100 A.D. postulated by Westcott, is probably correct. In recent years both conservative and liberal New Testament scholars have accepted

170

this as the probable date of the origin of John's Gospel. Even the radical critic Bultmann accepts this date.

The Sources of the Fourth Gospel
When Dean Streeter wrote his famous *The Four Gospels,* the quest for written sources for the Gospels was still the order of the day. Streeter held that the writer of the fourth Gospel had used at least Mark and Luke, and it was generally believed by some scholars that Mark had been utilized. G. H. Dodd in 1937 had come out for the use of Mark by the fourth Gospel but in 1954 he reversed his position. It was P. Gardner Smith who demonstrated to the satisfaction of many scholars that John was not dependent upon Mark. Bultmann in his commentary on John has rejected the dependence of the fourth Gospel on Mark. This change in attitude has been produced by the adoption of form criticism by a number of New Testament scholars who emphasize the oral tradition. It is as Fuller has written: "The trend today is to require a high percentage of verbal agreement plus agreement in order before concluding literary dependence."[1] Among current recognized John commentaries, Barrett is the only one who still holds that Mark and Luke were employed by John.

Rudolf Bultmann, professor at Tübingen, has proposed what some regard as a very interesting theory regarding the sources that were allegedly employed by the fourth Evangelist. The Tübingen professor postulated three different sources for the fourth Gospel. First, he distinguished a "Sigma Source" which might be distinguished by the siglum "S." This "Sign Source" is said to have in it many crass miracles and possibly other narrative miracles. Second, there was "a revelation discourses source" (Offenbahrungsreden) which Bultmann held had its origin in Gnosticism and was used in setting forth the kerygma. Bultmann maintains that he can distinguish between the material taken over from Gnosticism and that of the editor of the fourth Gospel. The Gnostic material was surprisingly enough written in Aramaic. Thirdly, Bultmann postulated another separate source, the editor's own version of the Passion narrative. This Passion narrative is said by Bultmann to be of greater value than that of Mark. What evidence does the German scholar have for his assumption of the use of Aramaic Gnostic sources? Bultmann has appealed to *The Odes of Solomon,* but these poems are in verse form and not in prose. This interpretation has made the author of the fourth Gospel merely a commentator and not a creative author in his own right. The German New Testament scholars Käsemann and Haenschen, have raised serious objections to this view of the alleged sources used for the fourth Gospel.

Since the discovery of the Dead Sea Scrolls (Qumran Scrolls) which were written between the years 275 B.C. and 66 A.D., some scholars have become convinced that the fourth Gospel has had contact with this sect that lived at Qumran. This religious group has been identified with the Essenes, already known from Josephus and certain early Christian writers. The Qumran sect believed in baptism and that men must experience a spiritual change in repentance. In John's Gospel a number of contrasts are mentioned that characterize those who believe or reject Christ. "Light" and "darkness" are two of the oppositional ideas portrayed in the fourth Gospel. In the Qumran writings similar passages set forth the difference between light and darkness as in John's Gospel. In the Qumran writings and the fourth Gospel there are references to the "children of light," and "to walking in the dark," as well as other expressions reminiscent of Johannine terminology. When the Dead Sea Scrolls were first discovered, the author of the fourth Gospel was said to have borrowed ideas from the Qumran document, known as *The War of the Sons of Light against the Sons of Darkness.* However, whatever similarities exist between the various Qumran writings and the fourth Gospel can also be explained by the fact that both writings came out of the same religious milieu which had its roots in the Old Testament. The contrast between the "righteous" and "the evil" constantly runs throughout the Psalms. The same statement also may be said relative to the claim put forth by certain scholars that both John the Baptist and Jesus borrowed some of the significant religious ideas from the sectaries of the Dead Sea Community. The Dead Sea Scrolls are valuable because they have established a link between the teachings of Jesus and the mainstream of Judaism, since these biblical manuscripts are nearly a thousand years older than the Hebrew manuscripts of the Middle Ages upon which the printed text of the Bible rests. In evaluating the relationship of the Qumran writings to those of the New Testament, it must not be forgotten that in the four Gospels we have inspired accounts of the deeds and saying of Jesus. These were written by eyewitnesses themselves (Matthew and John), and by Mark and Luke who had direct access to those who had been with Jesus during His public ministry and who, the early church writers said, associated with Peter and Paul, respectively.

The similarity of the Qumran writings would not rule out or make impossible a date as early as 60 A.D., which would completely demolish the non-apostolic second century date postulated by many critical scholars even to this day!

The Relationship of the Gospel of John
to the Three Epistles

Just as Christian tradition attributed the fourth Gospel to
the Apostle John, so the three Epistles have also been
ascribed to him. Some scholars contend that the author of
the fourth Gospel could not have written the three Epistles,
as traditionally held. They claim that theological concepts,
style and diction make it impossible to believe that the same
man who wrote John and Revelation could have penned the
seven chapters comprising the three Letters. A number of
critical scholars argue for the position that the three Epistles were composed between the years 100–110 A.D.

The principal purpose of I John was to combat the heresy
known as Docetism, by setting forth the "truth" about the
nature of Jesus Christ. As members of a Gnostic group, the
Docetists denied that Jesus could be true God and true man
at the same time. They proposed that salvation was to be
obtained by Gnosis, "knowledge" of divine mysteries. The
possessors of this "knowledge" were said to be incapable of
sinning and consequently were free from sin and any moral
obligations. They were also called Antinomians.

The Second Epistle is a plea for orthodoxy. It warns the
"elect lady" against Docetism and Antinomianism. The
Third Epistle, most likely written by the Apostle John,
warns Gaius of an opponent the author has encountered.

The arguments for the common authorship of the Gospel
and the Epistles are conclusive. Proof rests on the parallel
passages (e.g. John 1:1 and I John 1:1), common phrases,
such as "only-begotten," "born of God," common constructions (common use of conjunctions instead of subordinate
clauses), and common themes as *agape*, "love," *phos*,
"light," *zoe*, "life" and *meno* "to abide." There can be no
doubt that the same mind is at work in two different

situations. In the Gospel we have a profound study of Christ's incarnation written as an apologetic against the Gnostic heresy prevalent in Asia Minor. The Epistle of I John was also motivated by Gnostic heretical teaching. The differences between the Gospel and I John are to be accounted for by the various audiences and purposes that John the Apostle or Elder had in mind.

Modern Criticism and the Book of Revelation
Revelation, known in Greek as the Apocalypse, is the last book in the present order of the Greek New Testament, and it is the only book that belongs to the apocalyptic genre found in the Old Testament books of Isaiah, Joel, Ezekiel, Zechariah and Daniel. While there are apocalyptical passages in the Gospels and Epistles, Revelation is the only complete book that can be classified as "apocalyptical."

According to the interpretation of critical scholarship, the Book of Revelation has been influenced by the apocalyptical notions found in the apocalyptical works originating during the inter-testamental period. Daniel is supposed to have been the fountainhead for inter-testamental apocalypses like Enoch, Baruch and other books. Lowther Clark claims that "the political sphere was debarred to the prophets, who felt helpless against the heathen powers and were compelled to transfer their hopes from earth to heaven, from the present to the future. Ancient Semitic myths, which had been dormant in the time of the great prophets were revived and applied to the present emergency."[2] The writers of apocalypses are said to have inherited a certain form within which they had to formulate their presentation. According to critical scholars, apocalypses are alleged to have been written pseudonymously, such as Daniel and those of Enoch, Baruch, the Ezra Apocalypse, II Esdras

175

and others. Characteristic of apocalyptic writings is the supposition that God is sovereign and that ultimately He will intervene in catastrophic fashion to accomplish His good and perfect will. While it is true that some apocalyptic forms of literary genre are found in Revelation, this Johannine book is in a class by itself when compared with inter-testamental apocalypses. The Book of Revelation is not pseudonymous, but it has an author just as the book of Daniel in the Old Testament was written by the prophet Daniel. The author of Revelation is John who mentions himself in the opening verse of the Apocalypse. This book claims to be a book of prophecy. It is important to bear in mind that the Holy Spirit made use of a recognized form of literary genre to express to the churches through His servant John, "the things that must shortly come to pass" (1:3), so that the evils in the churches might be corrected and preparation made for historical events that were to affect these churches in the future. Therefore, Revelation is not to be considered a conventional apocalypse.

The Apostle John was a political prisoner on the Island of Patmos around 95 A.D. where the Emperor Domitian had banished him. The program of persecution that Domitian inaugurated, was more empire-wide than the Neronian persecution responsible for the beheading of Peter and Paul in Rome.

The author of Revelation describes himself as a "servant of Jesus Christ and companion in tribulation" (Rev. 1:9). Christian tradition has affirmed that this John was the author of the fourth Gospel and of the three Epistles. The belief that John the Apostle, the son of Zebedee, was the author of the last book of the New Testament dates back to Justin Martyr, about 140 A.D. and was also supported by Ireneus and others in the early church.

St. John's Writings in the Face of Criticism

Many modern scholars do not accept the identification of the John of Revelation with the Apostle John, the principal objection being the style of writing of the Apocalypse. The Greek of Revelation is in many respects different from that of the other Johannine writings. The unusual character of this book and the fact that the author sometimes shows scant respect for the normal rules of syntax, has prompted some scholars to deny the tradition of the early church which credited the Apostle John with the authorship of Revelation and designated Ephesus as its place of composition. Possibly because of the unique character of the revelations given to John, he used special constructions to emphasize the extraordinary content of that made known to him by Jesus Christ. Justin Martyr, in referring to the twentieth chapter of Revelation, stated that John, one of the Apostles of Christ, prophesied that those who believe in Christ should dwell in Jerusalem a thousand years. Ireneus quoted Revelation five times and named John as its author. Clement of Alexandria (200 A.D.) received the book as authentic Scripture and the Muratorian Fragment listed it as a part of the accepted canon by the end of the second century A.D.

The relationship of Revelation to the Apostle John was questioned by Dionysius of Alexandria (A.D. 231–256) on the grounds that the author unhesitatingly declared his name, whereas the author of the fourth Gospel did not and also that the style and vocabulary in Revelation were much different from that of the fourth Gospel and the Johannine Epistles. Dionysius concluded that the author of Revelation was a John, but not "the beloved disciple" John, the son of Zebedee. Eusebius in *Historia Ecclesia* (VII, 25) has given a lengthy quotation from Dionysius (VII, 39) in which there is a statement about two Johns in Ephesus, one who wrote

177

the Gospel and the other the Book of Revelation. However, the position of Eusebius was not accepted by the church fathers, nor does the internal evidence warrant two Johns. The "second John" is a shadowy figure who cannot be identified with any of the disciples of the Lord.

The so-called grammatical mistakes in Revelation can be logically explained as un-idiomatic translations of Hebrew or Aramaic expressions which would have been difficult to render into Greek. The very nature of the visions granted to John makes it difficult to describe them in human language. While it cannot be denied that there are striking divergences between Revelation and the other Johannine writings, the striking agreements must also be pointed out. The fourth Gospel and Revelation have the same view of man's predicament. Franzmann has written about this matter:

For the Gospel man as man is darkness and the world as world is under the judgment of God. This is what Revelation too declares with its judgmental riders, trumpets of doom, and bowls of wrath. If in the Gospel Jesus calls those who oppose Him children of the Devil and sees the world which hates Him under the dominion of this world, the devil, Revelation makes plain that the powers which persecute the church get their will and impetus from Satan.[3]

The fourth Gospel and the Apocalypse draw a clear line of distinction between the church and the world, and no compromise between truth and error, between darkness and light, between life and death, will be tolerated.

Some of the reasons for distinguishing between John the Apostle and John the Elder are the following: 1. An unlettered person could not have penned such a profound Gospel as the fourth Gospel. 2. It is unlikely that a fisher-

[3] *The Word of the Lord Grows.* Franzmann, Martin H. 1961, Concordia Publishing House. Used by permission of the publisher.

178

man's son would know and have access to the high priest. 3. An Apostle could not have referred to himself as the elder and author of the Apocalypse. 4. If the writer of the Gospel was John, it meant that he employed the writings of John Mark who was not an apostle, which is unlikely. In answer to these objections to the unity of authorship of the Epistles and Revelation, it may be stated: 1. "Unlettered" simply means lack of training in a rabbinical school but does not mean unlearned. 2. It is a wrong assumption that all fishermen were from the lower classes. 3. In I Pet. 5:1 the Apostle Peter speaks of himself as "an elder." 4. According to the critics Matthew the Apostle employed Mark as his source, and so in one instance critics are willing to admit that an Apostle employs other sources, but in John's case, he is not permitted to do so.

John the Apostle was one of the disciples who was given the promise on Maunday Thursday evening by Jesus, of the Holy Spirit, the Spirit that would guide them into all truth. The Johannine authorship of the fourth Gospel, the three Epistles and the Apocalypse would be consonant with this promise and would at the same time authenticate the divinity and inspired character of these five New Testament writings.

13
The Dependability of the Bible Today

Perhaps never before in history has there been a time when men had a greater need for a chart and compass to guide them in moral and spiritual matters than they do now. Today man faces tremendous issues in the moral and spiritual realms.

Political and social changes in our time are occurring with such rapidity as to cause consternation in the minds of many people. What events the future will bring is beyond prediction by any competent historian of our time. Change seems to be the only certainty. Human governments very often crumble under the impact of social forces, but God's government of the world does not change because God does not change. God abides, and man's need for God also remains. Man can approach this changeless God through a study of Holy Scriptures, the only book that was designed to have divine authority for the people of this world.

In the Old Testament the psalmist was certain that he had a reliable and dependable guide. In Psalm 119 the psalmist, who may have been Ezra, gave expression to a number of statements that assert a perfect revelation: "Thy

Word is very pure; therefore thy servant loveth it . . . The sum of thy word is truth; and every one of thy righteous ordinances endureth forever" (Ps. 119:140–160).[1] "Thy Word is a lamp unto my feet and a guide unto my path" (119:105).

It is reasonable to assume that God who has created man in His own image desires to communicate and give him direction for successful living and a meaningful existence. In nature and in the Bible God has given two revelations: a natural and a supernatural. Both reason and the Bible tell men that God is the source of all truth. Only a divine and omnipotent mind could originate truth, and this is the emphasis of the Scriptures. Thus the Old Testament describes the God of the Bible as "a God of truth" (Deut. 32:4). Yahweh is said to be "abundant in truth" (Ex. 34:6). Jesus asserted that "his word is truth" (John 17:17). Jesus said: "I am the way, the truth and the life" (John 14:6) and He told His disciples that He had come into the world to bear witness to the truth (John 18:37). Paul claimed that "the truth is in Jesus" (Eph. 4:21). The biblical writers were convinced that truth belonged to God. Thus the psalmist proclaimed: "His truth endureth to all generations" (Ps. 100:5): "His truth shall be thy shield and buckler" (Ps. 91:4). David asked God to "lead me in thy truth, and teach me" (Ps. 25:5).

It is the teaching of the Old and New Testament Scriptures that the truth may be known and apprehended regarding those matters that God would have men know. Paul describes the pathetic nadir of the intellectuals who are constantly learning but never able to come to a knowledge of the truth (II Tim. 3:7). Jesus promised His followers: "If you continue in my word, then are you my disciples indeed: and you shall know the truth, and the truth shall

181

make you free" (John 8:31–32). The Apostle John in writing to Gaius said: "I have no greater joy than to hear that my children walk in the truth" (III John 4). Paul calls the Christian to ward off error by using the armor of truth (Eph. 6:14).

Is the Bible dependable and trustworthy? Are its statements true as found in the original autographs? The Bible teaches that "the unspiritual man does not receive the gifts of the Spirit of God, for they are folly to him, and he is not able to understand them because they are spiritually discerned" (I Cor. 2:14 RSV). In order to accept the Bible as the Word of God it is necessary to be born again. The abnormal, depraved intellect of man must be remade by the Spirit. To become convinced of the Bible's truthfulness, the reader must first have been made a follower of Christ. Only by believing in Christ will it be possible for any person to become convinced of the veracity and trustworthiness of the Scriptures.

Christ is the key to understanding the Scriptures. Christ claimed that He came to bear witness of the truth (John 18:37). How did Christ regard the Old Testament Scriptures? He quoted often from them and constantly gave evidence that He regarded the Old Testament as God's errorless revelation. Frequently He proved a point by simply stating, "the Scripture says." Jesus also promised His Apostles on Maunday Thursday evening that He would send them the Holy Spirit who would guide them into all truth and that the Paraclete would bring back all things to their remembrance. In the high priestly prayer, Jesus prayed for His future church which would believe on Him through the Apostle's word.

Christ is the heart of the whole Scriptures. Of the Old Testament Jesus averred: "They testify of me" (John 5:39).

182

The Dependability of the Bible Today

Christ gives unity to the Bible. Frank Gaebelein explained this well when he wrote:

The Christological unity of the Bible requires the believer to take the stand with his Lord when it comes to the full reliability of the Word. Truth, although it has innumerable facets, belongs to God. And because Christ is one with God, he who said, "I am the truth," is the Lord of truth. And because Scripture finds its unity in him and is inspired by the Spirit whom he calls "the Spirit of truth," it is the Word of truth. Therefore, the Christological integration of the Bible guarantees its veracity.[2]

Christ told those who refused to accept His claims that if they would practice His doctrine, knowledge and veracity of His person and teaching would result for them. This challenge and offer continue to be made to all who will taste and see, and acceptance of this invitation by thousands upon thousands has resulted in belief in Christ's deity and in conviction of the truthfulness of His Word. The history of missions has furnished ample evidence for the Bible's dependability in promising to create a new heart and a new life in those persons who in repentance accept Jesus as their Lord and Master.

The issue of the truthfulness, dependability and trustworthiness of the Bible is interlocked with that of its divine inspiration. The Westminster Confession has stated it in this way:

The authority of the Holy Scripture, for which it ought to be believed and obeyed, dependeth not upon the testimony of any man or church, but wholly upon God (who is truth itself), author thereof; and therefore it is to be received, because it is the Word of God.[3]

When a person reads and accepts the claims of Scripture then the Holy Spirit will bear witness to the reader that the Bible is infallible truth and possesses divine authority.

Ultimately no historical and archaeological confirmation will establish the truth of the Bible's divine inspiration and consequent reliability. This conviction is produced only by the Holy Spirit.

The argument from fulfilled prophecy has always been advanced by apologists for the truthfulness of the Christian faith. The apostolic church in its missionary efforts stressed the truth that the Messianic prophecies in the Old Testament had been fulfilled in Jesus Christ. In his Pentecost sermon Peter claimed that David as a prophet had foretold the resurrection of the Christ and that this prediction was fulfilled when God raised Jesus from the dead (Acts 2:16, 25, 30, 31). This was the New Testament proof for the truthfulness of Christianity, namely, that the prophecies concerning God's Messiah had been realized in Jesus. When the Apostles employed this approach they were simply doing what God's prophets had done in the Old Testament. Thus the prophet in Isaiah 40–48 stresses the superiority of Yahweh over the Babylonian gods, because the latter could not predict events that were to transpire as Israel's God could and did. Large volumes have been written by biblical interpreters showing how in book after book, God's prophets announced historical happenings years before their occurrence. For example, Abraham was told twenty-five years before it came to pass that his wife Sarah would have a son. When Yahweh first met Moses He announced to the latter that He would deliver the Israelites out of a captivity that had lasted a long time, a prophecy that was fulfilled. In fact, Yahweh had told Abraham that his descendants would be strangers in Egypt for 400 years and then return to Canaan. Prophets such as Jeremiah and Ezekiel predicted the Babylonian captivity many years before Jerusalem was destroyed (587 B.C.) and many Judeans went into captivity.

184

Likewise, Jeremiah also announced the return from exile, a prophecy that was fulfilled. Nahum predicted the downfall of the Assyrian Empire and of its capital city, Nineveh.

In the Gospels Jesus predicted His capture, condemnation, resurrection and glorification. In the beginning of His public ministry Jesus announced: "Destroy this temple and in three days I will raise it up again," (John 2:19). This prophecy was fulfilled when Jesus arose on Easter morning. The unity of the two Testaments is established by the pattern of prophecy and fulfillment. Approximately 300 Old Testament prophecies relate to the Messiah and the coming of His kingdom. Of these 300 Messianic prophecies Culver has asserted: "They were like a piece of a jigsaw puzzle (except that each presented something distinct which a puzzle does not), more or less obscure until Jesus came and put them all in clear relation to one another by His career."[4]

The Bible is God's book and it exhibits a remarkable unity. It is difficult to account for this singular unity except on the basis of its divine authorship. David Burrell has expressed the argument for this proof as follows:

Here is a volume made up of sixty-six books, on a large variety of themes, composed of forty odd writers of various tongues and nationalities, writing at intervals along a period of sixteen hundred years and representing all degrees of racial development from semi-barbarism to the highest degree of culture; yet, strange to tell, these sixty-six books when bound together constitute a harmonious and consistent whole; yielding one system of doctrine, one code of ethics and, thus, one "rule of faith and practice" for all the children of men.[5]

While the Bible consists of two parts, the Old Testament is

[4]Used by permission. Moody Press, Moody Bible Institute of Chicago.

incomplete without the New Testament and the New Testament cannot properly be understood apart from the Old Testament. The Old Testament is perfectly accorded and symphonizes with the New Testament. The words of Augustine are true: "The New Testament is enfolded in the Old and the Old Testament is unfolded in the New."

That which gives especial unity to the two Testaments is the plan of salvation, having had its inception in Paradise and reaching its climax when on Calvary Christ bruised the serpent's head. Paul stated that the Old Testament, the Book of the Law was "a schoolmaster to bring us to Christ" (Gal. 3). Jesus said that the Old Testament testified of Him (John 5:39). Paul claimed that the Old Testament could make a person wise unto salvation by producing faith in Christ Jesus (II Tim. 3:15). It is supremely important to remember in the study of Scriptures that their nexus is the divine plan of salvation. To quote Burrell again:

Omit that and the whole fabric is reduced to threads and thrums. It is only with the Cross as our golden key that we so enter the Book as to perceive not only the unity of various parts but the profitableness of every part for some of the diverse uses of life.[6]

Another indication that the Bible is God's Word is the fact that only a small percentage of all books survive for more than a quarter of a century, a smaller percentage remain for a century, and only a very few last more than a thousand years. When we take cognizance of these facts and consider the circumstances under which the Bible has survived, then we begin to realize that the Bible must have God's power and protection behind it. Arthur Pink has stated this fact as follows:

When we bear in mind the fact that the Bible has been the special object of never ending persecution the *wonder* of the Bible's survival is changed into a *miracle*. . . . For 2,000 years man's hatred of the Bible has been persistent, determined, relentless and murderous. Every possible effort has been made to undermine faith in the inspiration and authority of the Bible and innumerable enterprises have been undertaken to consign it to oblivion. Imperial edicts have been issued to the effect that every known copy of the Bible should be destroyed, and when this measure failed to exterminate and annihilate God's Word then commands were given every person found with a copy of the Scriptures in his possession should be put to death. The very fact that the Bible has been so singled out for such relentless persecution causes us to wonder at such a unique phenomenon.[7]

Church history records many instances when attempts were made to prevent the distribution and reading of the Scriptures. During the early centuries the Roman emperors sought to exterminate the Bible, since it was the basis for Christian beliefs. Notably, Diocletian by a royal edict in 303 A.D. demanded that every copy of the Bible be surrendered and destroyed by fire. After the rise of the Waldenses the Church placed so many restrictions upon the reading of the Bible that people felt distrustful of the Scriptures. During the time of the Reformation the Roman Catholic Church put such severe restrictions on the reading of Protestant translations which had been rendered into all the major European languages and because they were told that they would not be properly able to understand it, people were discouraged from reading the Bible. The noted infidel Voltaire, who died in 1778, predicted that within a hundred years of his death Christianity would be extinct and the Bible unread. How successful Voltaire was in making the Bible obsolete may be seen from the fact that only twenty-five years after his death, the British and Foreign Bible Society was organized and the very presses that had published Voltaire's writings were used to publish Bibles.

How Dependable Is the Bible?

The twentieth century has also witnessed a great campaign to obliterate the Bible and its teachings. Un-Christian philosophies have endeavored by every possible means, either by force or kindly persuasion, to discredit the Bible and its teachings.

An attempt has also been made from within the church to downgrade the Bible by robbing it of its authority, by demoting the Scriptures to the level of other ancient books. If the Bible is used, it is depicted as not possessing supernatural authority. Christians who regard the Bible as God's Word realize that this is a device of the Evil One to undermine the Scriptures. In spite of all attempts to destroy the Bible as the Word of God, the complete Bible or a portion of it is being circulated in over 1,100 different languages and dialects. The Bible's indestructibility is another proof of its dependability.

A study of the character of the Bible's teachings reveals the truth that its contents have one divine author. A perusal of its basic and fundamental teachings will establish the conviction that its teachings are the embodiment of divine revelation. Consider the contents of Holy Scripture. Throughout the Old and New Testaments there is the recognition of the personality, unity and trinity of God. The various biblical books magnify the holiness and love of God. The biblical writers depict creation of all things, animate and inanimate as the direct work of God. Man is portrayed as made in the image and likeness of God. Man's fall is represented as a free revolt against the revealed will of God. The biblical authors describe sin as inexcusable, and that because of sin, man is under judgment and subject to eternal punishment unless he repents. Both Testaments not only teach that God is in sovereign control of the universe, but they also set forth God's great plan of salvation and the

188

conditions under which man may be a beneficiary of God's plan of love and mercy. The Bible delineates the purpose which God had for the children of Israel and for the Church to be established by Jesus Christ. Like no other sacred book, the Bible depicts the culmination of history, the second coming of Christ, the resurrection of all dead, the great judgment with eternal condemnation for those rejecting God and His Anointed One, and eternal blessedness to those receiving God's approval.

Since the Bible claims to be God's Word it is logical to expect its assertions to be in harmony with facts. Factual evidence is extremely important as a basis for the Gospel of Christ. The "Good News" to be good needs to be true; the assertions and teachings of the Bible must be found within a context of truth. Archaeology has played an important role in supporting the truthfulness of the Old and New Testaments. Jesus said to the Pharisees that "the very stones would cry out" in defense of Him. The many archaeological discoveries have for over a century been crying out in support of the facts of the Bible.

In years gone by infidels were eager to ridicule the Bible by insisting that individuals and nations then not known in secular history were erroneous. It was once claimed that King Sargon referred to in Isa. 20:1 was a fictional personality. However, in 1843 Botta began digging in Khorsabad and discovered the great palace of Sargon; and today we have many inscriptions from his palace.

As a result of archaeological discoveries Dr. A.A. McRae could write in 1948:

During the last few decades so many instances have occurred of remarkable agreement between a biblical statement and an archaeological discovery that this (critical) attitude toward the Bible has largely been changed, at least as far as first-hand scholars

189

are concerned. Today the Bible is recognized as a dependable historical source, even by many who do not accept its religious teachings, and its statements are generally treated with great respect by archaeologists, in view of the large number of instances where they have been shown to be remarkably accurate.[8]

While some scholars claim that archaeology should not be used to defend the Bible, the fact nevertheless remains that archaeology has become a great ally in showing the truthfulness of the Bible. Miller Burrows, a self-acknowledged theological liberal, is typical of a group of scholars who are manifesting a growing respect for the Bible. Thus he wrote: "On the whole, however, archaeological work has unquestionably strengthened confidence in the reliability of the scriptural record. More than one archaeologist has found his respect for the Bible increased by the experience of excavation in Palestine."[9]

Both H.H. Halley in his popular *Bible Handbook* and Merrill Unger in his *Bible Handbook* have listed at least a hundred places in the Old and New Testaments where archaeology has either illustrated the historicity of biblical accounts or verified their statements. The supernatural character of the Scripture's teachings are seen more and more as archaeological evidence becomes available.

While apologetical arguments are helpful in removing objections and doubts that have been produced by the detractors of the Bible, it must again be stressed that a Christian accepts the Bible as true and dependable because of his belief in Jesus Christ who has set the seal of His authority upon it. The Emmaus disciples were rebuked by the resurrected Christ as "fools, and slow of heart to believe all that the prophets have spoken" (Luke 24:25). Thus Christ gave the impression that anything contained in the Old Testament was to be accepted as true.

The Dependability of the Bible Today

Christian believers are convinced that their faith in the Bible's truthfulness is not resting upon wishful thinking and feeling, but that there is abundant evidence for the belief that the Bible is dependable. While only the Holy Spirit can convict a man and lead him into true faith, He can and does make use of the efforts of men in areas such as apologetics and archaeology. For those who already believe, the knowl ˙ edge of the infinite care evidenced in the transmission and preservation of the Bible leads to an even greater understanding of the power, wisdom and glory of God.

Notes

Chapter 1

[1]Edgar Work, *The Fascination of the Book* (New York: Fleming H. Revell & Co., 1906), pp. 7–8.

[2]As stated in *The Catalogue of the Biblical Seminary* in New York (Published at 235-49th Street, New York, N.Y., 1945), p. 63.

[3]M. B. Leavell, *Building a Christian Home* (Nashville: Sunday School Board of the Southern Baptist Convention, 1936), p. 76.

[4]Howard Tillman Kuist, "The Use of the Bible in Forming of Men," reprinted from the *Princeton Theological Seminary Bulletin,* June, 1944, p. 13.

[5]As quoted by J. T. Watts, *The Home and the Extension Department of the Sunday School* (Nashville: Sunday School Board of the Baptist Convention, 1930), p. 27.

[6]Clarence H. Benson, *A Popular History of Christian Education* (Chicago: Moody Press, 1943), pp. 327–328.

Chapter 2

[1]Bernard Ramm, *Protestant Biblical Interpretation* (Boston: W. A. Wilde Company, 1956), p. 101.

[2]Edgar Krentz, *Biblical Studies Today* (St. Louis: Concordia Publishing House, 1966), p. 32.

[3]E. Basil Redlich, *Form Criticism. Its Value and Limitations* (London: Duckworth, 1949), p. 18.

[4]Martin H. Franzmann, *The Word of the Lord Grows* (St. Louis: Concordia Publishing House, 1961), p. 217.

[5]Norman Perrin, *What Is Redaction Criticism?* (Philadelphia: Fortress Press, 1969), p. vii.

[6]*Ibid.*, p. 1.

192

Notes

Chapter 3

[1]B. Smalley, *The Study of the Bible in the Middle Ages* (New York: Philosophical Library, 1952), pp. 150–151.

Chapter 4

[1]Carl F. H. Henry, "Revelation, Special," in *Baker's Dictionary of Theology.* Editor-in-Chief, Everett F. Harrison (Grand Rapids: Baker Book House, 1960), p. 457.

[2]*Ibid.*, p. 458.

[3]Wick Broomall, *Biblical Criticism* (Grand Rapids: Zondervan Publishing House, 1957), p. 1.

[4]*Ibid.*

[5]Carl F. Henry, "Inspiration," in *Baker's Dictionary of Theology., op. cit.*, p. 288.

[6]Reinhold Seeberg, *Textbook of the History of Doctrines;* trans. by E. Hay (Grand Rapids: Baker Book House, 1954), I, p. 82.

[7]Henry, *op. cit*, p. 288.

Chapter 5

[1]F. F. Bruce, *The Book and the Parchments* (London: Pickering & Inglis, 1950), p. 170.

[2]Sir Frederick Kenyon, *The Bible and Archaeology* (New York and London: Harper and Brothers, Publishers, 1940), pp. 288–289.

[3]F. F. Bruce, *Second Thoughts on the Dead Sea Scrolls* (Grand Rapids: Wm. B. Eerdmans Publishing Company, 1956), pp. 61–62.

[4]Miller Burrows, *The Dead Sea Scrolls* (New York: The Viking Press, 1955), p. 304.

[5]Francis Pieper, *Christian Dogmatics* (St. Louis: Concordia Publishing House, 1950), I, p. 340. Used by Permission of the publisher.

Chapter 6

[1]Merrill F. Unger, *Introductory Guide to the Old Testament* (Grand Rapids: Zondervan Publishing House, 1950), pp. 227–228.

[2]John L. McKenzie, *Dictionary of the Bible* (Milwaukee: The Bruce Publishing Company, 1965), p. 360.

[3]*Ibid.*

[4]C. R. North, "History," in *The Interpreter's Dictionary of the Bible*, ed. George Buttrick (New York: Abingdon Press, 1962), II, p. 608.

[5]McKenzie, *op. cit.*, p. 361.

[6]C. Epping, "Historiography," in *Encyclopedic Dictionary of the Bible*, ed. Louis F. Hartmann (New York: Toronto, and London: McGraw-Hill Book Company, 1963), p. 1010.

[7]Claus Westermann, *A Thousand Years and A Day* (Philadelphia: Fortress Press, 1962), p. 2.

Notes

[8]A. H. McNeile, "Moses," James Hastings, *Dictionary of the Bible*, revised edition by Frederick C. Grant and H. H. Rowley (New York: Charles Scribner's Sons, 1963), p. 677.

[9]Meredith G. Kline, "Is the History of the Old Testament Accurate?" in Howard F. Vos (ed) *Can I Trust My Bible?* (Chicago: Moody Press, 1963), p. 135.

Chapter 8

[1]Harry Ranstoun, *The Old Testament Wisdom Books and Their Teaching* (London: Epworth Press, 1940), p. 19.

[2]David E. Robison, "The Wisdom Literature of the Old Testament," in *Old Testament Commentary*, eds. Herbert C. Alleman and Elmer Flack (Philadelphia: Muhlenberg Press, 1948), p. 76.

[3]*The Holy Bible*. Sponsored by the Episcopal Committee of Confraternity of Christian Doctrine (Patterson, N.J.: St. Anthony Guild Press, 1957), II, p.411.

[4]A. S. Hooke, "Wisdom," *Dictionary of the Bible*. Edited by James Hastings. Revised Edition by Frederick C. Grant and H. H. Roley, 1963. p. 1040.

[5]David E. Robison, "The Wisdom Literature of the *Old Testament Commentary*" edited by Herbert C. Allemann and Elmer E. Flack (Philadelphia: Muhlenberg Press, 1948), p. 81.

Chapter 9

[1]Merrill F. Unger, *Unger's Bible Dictionary* (Chicago: Moody Press, 1957), p. 891.

[2]D. J. McCarthy, "Prophetism," in *New Catholic Encyclopedia*, 1965, XI, 870.

[3]Bruce Vawter, *Introduction to the Prophetical Books* (Collegeville, Minn.: The Liturgical Press, 1965), p. 5.

[4]Wilfred J. Harrington, *Record of the Promise* (Chicago: Prioriy Press, 1965), p. 178.

[5]*Ibid.*, p. 178.

Chapter 10

[1]Kirsopp Lake, *Eusebius. The Ecclesiastical History* (New York: C. P. Putnam's Sons, 1926), I, pp. 291–292.

[2]J.E.I. Oulton, *Eusebius. The Ecclesiastical History* (Cambridge, Mass.: Harvard University Press, 1942), II, p. 49.

[3]Merrill C. Tenney, "Gospels," in *The Zondervan Pictorial Bible* Dictionary, ed. Merril C. Tenney (Grand Rapids: Zondervan Publishing House, 1963), p. 320.

[4]Floyd V. Filson, "Form Criticism," in *Twentieth Century Encyclopedia*

of Religious Knowledge, ed. Lefferts A. Loetscher (Grand Rapids: Baker Book House, 1955), I, p. 436.

[6]Cited by R. A. Egon Hessel, "Is Christianity a Myth?" In *The Christian Century,* Sept. 3, 1952, p. 993.

[7]Filson, *op. cit.,* p. 437.

Chapter 11

[1]Reginald H. Fuller, *The New Testament in Current* Study (New York: Charles Scribner's Sons, 1962), pp. 11–12.

[2]J. B. Lightfoot, *St. Paul's Epistle to the Galatians* (London: Macmillan and Company, 1876), pp. 43-44.

[3]Simon Greenleaf, *An Examination of the Testimony of the Four Evangelists* (London, 1847), p. 7.

Chapter 12

[1]Reginald Fuller, *The New Testament in Current Study* (New York: Charles Scribner's Sons, 1962), pp. 11-12.

[2]W. K. Lowther Clarke, *Concise Bible Commentary* (New York: The Macmillan Company, 1953), p.935.

[3]Martin H. Franzmann, *The Word of the Lord Grows* (St. Louis: Concordia Publishing House, 1961), p. 283. Used by permission of the publisher.

Chapter 13

[1]King James Version.

[2]Frank E. Gaebelein, "The Unity of the Bible," in Carl F. Henry (ed) *Revelation and the Bible* (Grand Rapids: Baker Book House, 1958), p. 398.

[3]Phillip Schaff, *The Creeds of Christendom* (New York: Harper & Brothers, 1877), III, p. 602.

[4]Robert D. Culver, "Were the Old Testament Prophecies Really Prophetic?" in Howard F. Vos (ed.) *Can I Trust My Bible?* (Chicago: Moody Press, 1963), p. 109.

[5]David James Burrell, *Why I Believe the Bible* (New York: Fleming H. Revell and Company, 1917), p. 26.

[6]*Ibid.,* p. 30.

[7]Arthur W. Pink, *The Divine Inspiration of the Bible* (Swengel, Pa.: Bible Truth Depot, 1917), pp. 113-114.

[8]Allan A. McRae, "The Relation of Archaeology to the Bible," in *Modern Science and the Christian Faith* (Wheaton, Ill.: Van Kempen Press, 1948), p. 266.

[9]Millar Burrows, *What Mean These Stones?* (New Haven: American Schools of Oriental research, 1941), p. 1.

Selected Bibliography

1. Who's Listening?

Benson, Clarence H. *A Popular History of Christian Education.* Chicago: Moody Press, 1943. cf. especially pp. 294–332.

De Wolf, L. Harold. *Trends and Frontiers in Religous Thought.* Nashville: National Methodist Student Movement, 1955.

Gordon, Ernst. *The Leaven of the Pharisees.* Chicago: The Bible Colportage Assn., 1926. cf. especially pp. 101–137; 159–211; 212257.

Hedegard, David. *Ecumenism and the Bible.* London: Banner of Truth Trust, 1964. cf. especially pp. 30–51.

Henry, Carl F. H. *Fifty Years of Protestant Theology.* Boston: W. A. Wilde Company, 1950.

Machen, J. Gresham. *Christianity and Liberalism.* New York: The Macmillan Company, 1923.

Nash, Arnold S. *Protestant Thought in the Twentieth Century.* New York: The Macmillan Company, 1951.

Richardson, Alan. *Relgion in Contemporary Debate.* Philadelphia: The Westminster Press, 1966.

Smith, Wilbur M. *Therefore Stand.* Boston: W. A. Wilde Co., 1945. Cf. especially pp. 1–202.

2. What Is Valid Biblical Criticism?

Beardslee, William A. *Literary Criticism of the New Testament.* Philadelphia: Fortress Press, 1970.

Bruce, F. F. "Biblical Criticism." *The New Bible Dictionary.* Grand Rapids: Wm. B. Eerdmans Publishing Company, 1962.

Bruce, F. F. "Criticism and Faith." *Christianity Today.* V. November 21, 1960, pp. 145–148.

Grobel, K. "Biblical Criticism." *The Interpreter's Dictionary of the Bible.* A–D. New York and Nashville: The Abingdon Press, 1962.

Hahn, Herbert F. *The Old Testament in Modern Research. With a Survey of Recent Literature,* by Horace Hummel. Philadelphia: Fortress Press, 1966.

Knox, John. *Criticism and Faith.* New York and Nashville: Abingdon-Cokesbury Press, 1957.

Koch, Klaus. *The Growth of the Biblical Tradition. The Form-Critical Method.* Translated by S. M. Cupitt from the second German edition. New York: Charles Scribner's Sons, 1969.

Krentz, Edgar. *Biblical Studies Today.* St. Louis: Concordia Publishing House, 1966.

Ladd, George Eldon. *The New Testament and Criticism.* Grand Rapids: Wm. B. Eerdmans Publishing Company, 1967.

Manley, G. T. *The New Bible Handbook.* Chicago and Toronto: The Inter-Varsity Christian Fellowship, 1949, pp. 40–56.

McNight, Edgar V. *What Is Form Criticism?* Philadelphia: Fortress Press, 1969.

Perrin, Norman. *What Is Redaction Criticism?* Philadelphia: Fortress Press, 1969.

Rowley, H. H. "Biblical Criticism." *Chambers Encyclopedia,* 1964. Vol. II.

Tenney, Merrill C. "The Limits of Biblical Criticism." *Christianity Today.* V, November 21, 1960, pp. 141–2, 144.

3. Biblical Criticsm throughout the Ages.

DeVries, S. J. "Biblical Criticism, History of." *The Interpreter's Dictionary of the Bible,* A–D. Edited by George Buttrick. New York and Nashville: Abingdon Press, 1962.

Grant, Robert. *The Bible in the Church.* New York: The Macmillan Company, 1948.

Grant, Robert. McNeill and Terrien, Samuel. "History of the Interpretation of the Bible: I. Ancient Period, II Medieval and Reformation Period and III Modern Period." *The Interpreter's Bible.* I. New York and Nashville: Abingdon-Cokesbury Press, 1952.

Nineham, D. E. *The Church's Use of the Bible. London: SPCK, 1963*

Piper, Otto A. "The Bible." *Collier's Encyclopedia.* 1961 Vol. III.

Roehrs, W. "Higher Criticism" *Lutheran Cyclopedia.* Edited by Erwin L. Lueker. St. Louis: Concordia Publishing House, 1954.

Steinmann, Jean. *Biblical Criticism.* Translated from the French by J. R. Foster. New York: Hawthorn Publishers, 1958.

Walvoord, John., ed. *Inspiration and Interpretation.* Grand Rapids: Wm. B. Eerdmans Publishing Company, 1957.

Selected Bibliography

4. Revelation, Inspiration and Biblical Criticism.

Written from the Critical Viewpoint:
Abba, Raymond. *The Nature and Authority of the Bible*. Philadelphia: Muhlenberg Press, 1958.
Beegel, Dewey M. *The Inspiration of Scripture*. Philadelphia: The Westminster Press, 1963.
Charlier, Dom Celestine. *The Christian Approach to the Bible*. Westminster, Md.: The Newman Press, 1963.
Hooke, S. H. *What Is the Bible?* London: SCM Press, 1948.
Shokel, Luis Alonso. *Understanding Biblical Research*. Translated by Peter J. N. McCord. New York: Herder and Herder, 1963.
Written from the Conservative Viewpoint:
Broomall, Wick. *Biblical Criticism*. Grand Rapids: Zondervan Publishing House, 1957.
Custer, Steward. *Does Inspiration Demand Inerrancy?* Nutley, N.J.: The Craig Press, 1968.
Engelder, T. E. *Scripture Cannot Be Broken*. St. Louis: Concordia Publishing House, 1944.
Harris, R. Laird. *The Inspiration and Canonicity of the Bible*. Grand Rapids: Zondervan Publishing House, 1957.
Henry, Carl F. ed. *Revelation and the Bible in Contemporary Thought*. Grand Rapids: Baker Book House, 1958.
Montgomery, John Warwick, *Crisis in Lutheran Theology*. I. Grand Rapids: Baker Book House, 1967. Cf. especially pp. 15-44.
Packer, James I. *Revelation and Inspiration*. Philadelphia: The Westminster Press, 1966.
Pinnock, Clark. *A Defense of Biblical Infallibility*. Philadelphia: Presbyterian and Reformed Publishing Company, 1967.
Tenney, Merrill C. *The Bible-The Living Word of God*. Grand Rapids: Zondervan Publishing House, 1968.
Warfield, Benjamin. *Revelation and Inspiration*. New York: Oxford University Press, 1927. especially pp. 395-425.
Young, Edward J. *Thy Word is Truth*. Grand Rapids: Wm. B. Eerdmans Publishing Company, 1957.

5. The Reliability of the Biblical Text.

Ap-Thomas, D. R. *A Primer of Old Testament Text Criticism*. Philadelphia: Fortress Press, 1966.
Birdsall, J. N. "The New Testament Text." *Cambridge History of the Bible*. Vol. I: From the Beginnings to Jerome. Edited by Ackroyd and Evans. Cambridge: At the University Press, 1970.

Selected Bibliography

Bruce, F. F. *The Books and the Parchments*. London: Pickering & Inglis, 1950.

Burrows, Millar. *The Dead Sea Scrolls*. New York: The Viking Press, 1956. cf. especially pp. 73-126.

Flack, Elmer: Metzger, Bruce: and others. *The Text, Canon, and Principal Versions of the Bible*. Grand Rapids: Baker Book House, 1956.

Geisler, Norman L. and Nix, William E. *A General Introduction to the Bible*. Chicago: Moody Press, 1968. cf. Especially pp. 235-393.

Greenlee, J. Harold. *Introduction to New Testament Textual Criticism*. Grand Rapids: Wm. B. Eerdmans Publishing Company, 1964.

Kenyon, Frederick. *Our Bible and the Ancient Manuscripts*. Revised by A. W. Adam, New York: Harper & Brothers, Publishers, 1958.

Lightfoot, Neil R. *How We Got Our Bible*. Grand Rapids: Baker Book House, 1963.

Price, Ira Maurice. *The Ancestry of Our English Bible*. Third revised edition by William A. Irwin. New York: Harper & Brothers, 1956. cf. especially pp. 13-224.

Taylor, Vincent. *The Text of the New Testament*. London: Macmillan & Co., Ltd., 1961.

6. How "Historical" Is Old Testament History?

Written from a Critical Viewpoint:

Barkley, William. Ed. *The Bible and History*. New York and Nashville: Abingdon Press, 1968, cf. especially pp. 19-152.

Clarke, W. K. Lowther. *Concise Bible Commentary*. New York: The Macmillan Company, 1953. cf. especially pp. 301-307.

Mackenzie, R. A. F. *Faith and History in the Old Testament*. New York: Macmillan Company, 1963.

McKenzie, John L. *Dictionary of the Bible*. Milwaukee: The Bruce Publishing Company, 1965. cf. especially pp. 360-363.

North, C. R. *The Interpretation of Old Testament History*. London: Epworth Press, 1953.

Sullivan, Kathryn. *God's Words and Work*. Collegeville, Minn.: The Liturgical Press, 1958.

Written From a Conservative Viewpoint

Aalders, G. Ch. "The Historical Literature of the Old Testament." Edited by E. Davidson. *The New Bible Commentary*. Grand Rapids: Wm. B. Eerdmans Publishing Company, 1953.

Allis, Oswald T. *The Five Books of Moses*. Philadelphia: Presbyterian and Reformed Publishing Company, 1942.

Anderson, Francis I. "The Historical Books." Edited by Carl F. Henry. *The Biblical Expositor*. Philadelphia: A. J. Holman Company, 1960. I

Selected Bibliography

Hamilton, Floyd E. *The Basis of the Christian Faith.* Third Revised Edition; New York: Harper and Brothers, 1946. cf. especially pp. 164–193.

Harrison, R. K. *Introduction to the Old Testament.* Grand Rapids: William B. Eerdmans Publishing Company, 1969. cf. especially pp. 291–348.

Kline, Meredith. "Is the History of the Old Testament Accurate?" Edited by Howard F. Vos. *Can I Trust My Bible?* Chicago: Moody Press, 1963.

Manley, G. T., ed. *The New Bible Handbook.* Chicago: and Toronto: The Intervarsity Christian Fellowship, 1949. cf. especially pp. 77–114.

Pieters, Albertus. *Can We Trust Bible History?* Grand Rapids: Wm. B. Eerdmans Publishing Company, 1954.

Wilson, Robert D. *A Scientific Investigation of the Old Testament.* With revision by Edward A. Young. Chicago: Moody Press, 1959. cf. especially pp. 131–158.

7. Literary Criticism and Biblical Poetry

Written from a Critical Viewpoint

Barth, Christoph F. *Introduction to the Psalms.* Translated by R. A. Wilson. New York: Charles Scribner's Sons, 1966.

Drijvers, Pius. *The Psalms. Their Structure and Meaning.* New York: Herder and Herder, 1965.

Günkel, Herman. *The Psalms. A Form-Critical Introduction.* Translated by Thomas M. Horner. Philadelphia: Fortress Press, 1967.

Guthrie, Harvey H. *Israel's Sacred Songs.* A Study of Dominant Themes. New York: The Seabury Press, 1966.

Robinson, Theodore H. *The Poetry of the Old Testament.* London: Duckworth, 1947.

Written from a Conservative Viewpoint:

Bruce, F. F. "The Poetry of the Old Testament." *The New Bible Commentary.* Edited by F. Davidson. Grand Rapids: Wm. B. Eerdmans Publishing Company, 1962.

Blackwood, Andrew W. "The Poetical Books." *The Biblical Expositor.* Edited by Carl F. Henry. Vol. II. Philadelphia: A. J. Holman Company, 1960.

Harrison, R. H. *Introduction to the Old Testament.* Grand Rapids: Wm. B. Eerdmans Publishing Company, 1969. cf. especially pp. 963–1004.

Leupold, H. C. *Exposition of the Psalms.* Columbus: The Wartburg Press, 1959. cf. especially pp. 1–29.

8. Higher Criticism and the Wisdom Literature.

Written from a Critical Viewpoint:

Blank, S. H. "Wisdom." *The Interpreter's Dictionary of the Bible.* Edited by George Buttrick. Vol. 4.

Selected Bibliography

Murphy, Roland E. *Seven Books of Wisdom*. Milwaukee: The Bruce Publishing Company, 1960.

Paterson, John. *The Book That Is Alive. Studies in Old Testament Life and Thought As Set Forth by the Hebrew Sages*. New York: Charles Scribner's Sons, 1954.

Rankin, O. S. *Israel's Wisdom Literature*. Edinburg: T. & T. Clarke, 1954.

Robison, David E. "The Wisdom Literature of the Old Testament." *Old Testament Commentary*. Edited by H. C. Alleman, and E. E. Flack. Philadelphia: The Muhlenberg Press, 1948.

Written from a Conservative Viewpoint:

Bruce, F. F. and Davidson. "The Wisdom Literature." *The New Bible Commentary*. Edited by F. Davidson. Grand Rapids: Wm. B. Eerdmans Publishing Company, 1962.

Harrison, R. K. *Introduction to the Old Testament*. Grand Rapids: William B. Eerdmans Publishing Company, 1969. cf. especially pp. 1004–1046.

Schultz, Samuel J. *The Old Testament Speaks*. New York: Harper & Brothers, 1960. cf. especially pp. 279–299.

Weidner, Revere Franklin. *Biblical Theology of the Old Testament*. Chicago: Wartburg Publishing House, 1896. cf. especially pp. 315–335.

9. True or False Prophecy

Written from the Critical Viewpoint:

Lindblom, J. *Prophecy in Ancient Israel*. Philadelphia: Fortress Press, 1965.

Kuhl, Curt. *The Prophets of Israel*. Richmond, Virginia: John Knox Press, 1960.

Murphy, Dennis J. *His Servants the Prophets*. Collegeville, Minn.: The Liturgical Press, 1962.

Robinson, T. H. *Prophecy and the Prophets*. London: Duckworth, 1923.

Westermann, Claus. *Basic Forms of Prophetic Speech*. Translated by Hugh Clayton. Philadelphia: The Westminster Press, 1962.

Written from a Conservative Viewpoint:

Ellison, H. L. *Men Spoke from God*. Grand Rapids: Wm. B. Eerdmans Publishing Company, 1952.

Freeman, Hobart E. *An Introduction to the Old Testament Prophets*. Chicago: Moody Press, 1968.

Grider, J. Kenneth. "The Prophetical Books," *The Biblical Expositor*. Edited by Carl F. Henry. II Philadelphia: A. J. Holman Company, 1960.

Motyer, J. A. "Prophecy, Prophets." *The New Bible Dictionary*. Edited by F. Davidson. Grand Rapids: Wm. B. Eerdmans Publishing Company, 1962.

Young, Edward E. *My Servants the Prophets*. Grand Rapids: Wm. B. Eerdmans Publishing Company, 1955.

Selected Bibliography

10. Can the First Three Gospels Be Trusted?

Written from a Critical Viewpoint:
Barclay, William. *The First Three Gospels.* London: SCM Press, 1966.
Briggs, R. C. *Interpreting the Gospels.* New York and Nashville: Abingdon Press, 1969.
Davies, W. D. *Invitation to the New Testament.* New York: Garden City: Doubleday & Company, Inc., 1966. cf. especially pp. 75-232.
Grant, Robert M. *A Historical Introduction to the New Testament.* New York and Evanston: Harper & Row, Publishers, 1963. cf. especially pp. 105-143.
Spivey, Robert A. and Smith, D. Moody. *Anatomy of the New Testament.* New York: The Macmillan Company, 1969. cf. especially pp. 61-238.
Vawter, Bruce. *The Four Gospels* New York, Garden City: Doubleday & Company, 1967.
Written from a Conservative Viewpoint:
Bruce, F. F. *Are the New Testament Documents Reliable?* London: The Inter-Varsity Fellowship of Evangelical Unions, 1945. cf. especially pp. 28-74.
Franzmann, Martin H. *The Word of the Lord Grows.* St. Louis: Concordia Publishing House, 1961. cf. especially pp. 168-218.
Guthrie, Donald. *New Testament Introduction.* The Gospels and Acts. Chicago: Inter-Varsity Press, 1965. cf. especially pp.11-211.
Harrison, Everett F. *Introduction to the New Testament.* Grand Rapids: Wm. B. Eerdmans Publishing Company, 1964. cf. especially pp. 131-200.
Henry, Carl F. H., ed. *Jesus of Nazareth: Saviour and Lord.* Grand Rapids: Wm. B. Eerdmans Publishing Company, 1966.
Stonehouse, Ned B. *Origins of the Synoptic Gospels.* Grand Rapids: Wm. B. Eerdmans Publishing Company, 1963.
Westcott, Brooke Foss. *An Introduction to the Study of the Gospels.* London: Macmillan & Company, 1899.

11. Letters as Literature

Written from a Critical Viewpoint:
Davies, W. D. *Invitation to the New Testament.* Garden City, N.Y.: Doubleday & Company, Inc., 1966. cf. especially pp. 232-372.
Feine, Paul; Behm, John; and Kümmel, Wener George. *Introduction to the New Testament.* Trans. by A. J. Mattick. New York and Nashville: Abingdon Press, 1965. cf. especially pp. 175-315.
Fuller, Reginald H. *The New Testament in Current Study.* New York: Charles Scribner's Sons, 1962. cf. especially pp. 54-70.

Selected Bibliography

Henshaw, T. *New Testament Literature*. London: George Allen and Unwin Ltd., 1952. cf. especially pp. 203-400.

Selby, Donald Joseph. *Toward the Understanding of Paul*. Englewood Cliffs, N.J.: Prentice-Hall, Inc., 1962. cf. especially pp. 235-295.

Written from a Conservative Viewpoint:

Barker, Glenn W.; Lane, William L.; and Michael, J. Ramsey. *The New Testament Speaks*. New York: Harper & Row, 1969. cf. especially pp. 143-247; 308-361.

Ellis, E. Earle. *Paul and His Recent Interpreters*. Grand Rapids: Wm. B. Eerdmans Publishing Company, 1961.

Guthrie, Donald *Introduction to the New Testament. The Epistles of Paul*. Chicago: Inter-Varsity Press, 1963.

Harrison, Everett F. *Introduction to the New Testament*. Grand Rapids: Wm. B. Eerdmans Publishing Company, 1964. cf. especially pp. 238-401.

Hiebert, D. Edmond. *An Introduction to the Pauline Epistles*. Chicago: Moody Press, 1954.

12. St. John's Writings in the Fact of Criticism

Written from a Critical Viewpoint:

Colwell, Ernst Cadman. *John Defends the Gospel*. Chicago: Willett, Clark & Company, 1936.

Feine, Paul; Behm, Johannes; Kummel Wener George. *Introduction to the New Testament*. Trans. by A. J. Mattil, New York and Nashville: Abingdon Press, 1965. cf. especially pp. 176-315.

Fuller, Reginald H. *The New Testament in Current Study*. New York: Charles Scribner's Sons, 1962. cf. especially pp. 101-132.

Grant, Robert M. *A Historical Introduction to the New Testament*. New York and Evanston: Harper & Row, Publishers, 1963. cf. especially pp. 148-162; 23-240.

Henshaw, T. *New Testament Literature*. London: George Allen and Unwin Ltd., 1952. cf. especially pp. 401-422.

Written From a Conservative Viewpoint:

Barker, Glen W.; Lane, William L.; Michaels, J. Ramsey. *The New Testament Speaks*. New York and Evanston: Harper & Row, Publishers, 1969. cf. especially pp. 362-380; 385-425.

Franzmann, Martin H. *The Word of the Lord Grows*. St. Louis: Concordia Publishing House, 1961. cf. especially pp. 247-285.

Harrison, Everett. *Introduction to the New Testament*. Grand Rapids: Wm. B. Eerdmans Publishing Company, 1964. cf. especially pp. 200-221; 411-451.

Tenney, Merrill C. *The New Testament. An Historical and Analytical*

Selected Bibliography

Survey. Grand Rapids: Wm. B. Eerdman's Publishing Company, 1953. cf. especially pp. 197–212; 393–416.

13. The Dependability of the Bible Today

Anderson, Stanley E. *Our Dependable Bible*. Grand Rapids; Baker Book House, 1960.

Bruce, F. F. *The Defense of the Gospel in the New Testament*. Grand Rapids: Wm. B. Eerdmans Publishing Company, 1953.

Burrell, David James. *Why I Believe the Bible*. New York: Fleming H. Revell Company, 1917.

Craig, Samuel G. *Christianity Rightly So-called*. Philadelphia: The Presbyterian and Reformed Publishing Company, 1946.

Gerstner, John H. *Reasons for Faith*. Grand Rapids: Baker Book House, 1967.

Hamilton, Floyd E. *The Basis of Christian Faith*. A Modern defense of the Christian Religion. 3rd Rev. Edition; New York: Harper & Brothers, 1946.

Johnson, Douglas. *The Christian and His Bible*. Grand Rapids: Wm. B. Eerdmans Publishing Company, 1953.

Montgomery, John Warwick. *Where Is History Going?* Grand Rapids: Zondervan Publishing House, 1969. cf. especially pp. 15–74.

Saanivaara, Uuras. *Hath God Saith? Who Is Right—God or the Liberals?* Minneapolis: Osterhus Publishing House, Inc., 1967.

Vos, Howard F. ed. *Can I Trust My Bible?* Chicago: Moody Press, 1963.